ONE LIFE : NEVER TOO LATE

Discover your Potential at any Age

Stories of triumph and transformations

Saurabh Sharma

ASTITVA PRAKASHAN

Parijat Heights, Bilaspur, Chhattisgarh 495001

India

First published by Astitva Prakashan 2025

ISBN: 978-93-7002-891-3

The views and opinions expressed in this book are the author's own. The facts contained herein were reported to be true as on the date of publication by the author to the publishers of the book, and the publishers are not in any way liable for their accuracy or veracity.

astitva prakashan

"To my loving family, who have supported me every step of the way."

Contents

Part Three

Igniting Your Own Potential

Introduction

We live in a society obsessed with timelines. From the moment we enter school, we're bombarded with expectations. Graduate by a certain age, land a stable job by another, marry, buy a house, have children - all within a prescribed window of time. These unspoken rules create a sense of urgency, a feeling that we're constantly racing against the clock. We're told that youth is synonymous with opportunity, that our prime years are reserved for achieving our dreams. But what happens when life takes unexpected turns? What if our passions ignite later in life? What if we find ourselves yearning for something more long after we've supposedly passed our "peak"?

This societal pressure to conform to a predetermined timeline can be incredibly limiting. It can lead to feelings of anxiety, inadequacy, and a sense of urgency that often hinders rather than helps. We may feel pressured to make hasty decisions, to pursue paths that don't truly fulfill us, simply because we feel we are "running out of time." This can lead to a life of unfulfillment, a constant sense of "should haves" and "could haves," and a nagging feeling that we've somehow missed our chance for happiness and success.

However, the reality is that life rarely unfolds according to a pre-set script. Unexpected events, unforeseen circumstances, and the evolution of our own interests and desires can significantly alter our paths. What seemed like the "right" course of action at one point in our lives may no longer resonate with us as we grow and evolve.

Furthermore, the notion that our prime years are limited to youth is a significant misconception. While youth offers certain advantages, such as physical energy and perhaps a greater capacity for risk-taking, it's far from the only time in life when we can achieve greatness. In fact, many individuals find that their most creative and fulfilling periods occur later in life. With age comes wisdom, experience, and a deeper understanding of oneself and the world. These qualities can be invaluable assets in pursuing personal and professional goals.

It's crucial to remember that life is a journey, not a race. There is no single "right" path or a predetermined timeline for achieving success. Our paths will inevitably be unique and filled with unexpected twists and turns. The key is to embrace these detours, to listen to our inner voice, and to pursue our passions with authenticity and joy, regardless of our age.

This book is a testament to the enduring power of the human spirit, a celebration of those who defied conventional wisdom and achieved extraordinary feats not in their youth, but in the later chapters of their lives. ***"One Life, Never Too Late"*** explores the remarkable journeys of individuals who found their purpose, ignited their passions, and achieved remarkable success long after society deemed them past their prime. Their stories are a powerful reminder that it is never too late to pursue our dreams, to reinvent ourselves, or to leave our mark on the world.

The narrative of aging in our society is often one of decline. We're bombarded with images of youthful vitality, while the process of growing older is often portrayed as a slow descent into irrelevance. We're told that our physical and mental capacities diminish with age, that our opportunities dwindle, and that our best years are behind us. This pervasive narrative can be incredibly damaging, leading to feelings of despair, resignation, and a sense of lost potential. Many people internalize these messages, believing that their time for greatness has passed. They settle for less than they're capable of, silencing the whispers of their own ambitions.

But the stories within these pages tell a different story. They reveal the incredible potential that lies dormant within each of us, regardless of age. They demonstrate that experience, wisdom, and a lifetime of accumulated knowledge can be powerful assets in the pursuit of our goals. In fact, for many of the individuals featured in this book, it was precisely their life experiences that provided the foundation for their later-life successes. They had weathered storms, learned from setbacks, and developed a deep understanding of themselves and the world around them. This hard-earned wisdom became the fuel that propelled them towards their extraordinary achievements.

This book is not about denying the realities of aging. It's not about pretending that physical or mental changes don't occur. Instead, it's about reframing our perspective on aging, recognizing it not as a period of decline, but as a period of transformation, growth, and renewed possibility. It's about understanding that our potential doesn't diminish with age, it simply evolves.

The individuals profiled in ***"One Life, Never Too Late"*** come from diverse backgrounds and pursued vastly different paths. Some found success in the world of business, building empires from the ground up later in life. Others discovered their artistic talents in their golden years, creating works of beauty and inspiration that resonated with audiences worldwide. Some pursued athletic feats that defied the limits of age, pushing the boundaries of human endurance and proving that age is just a number. And still others dedicated their later years to philanthropic pursuits, making a profound impact on their communities and the world at large.

These stories are not anomalies. They are not exceptions to the rule. They are powerful examples of what is possible when we refuse to be defined by age. They demonstrate that the human spirit is capable of extraordinary resilience, that passion can ignite at any stage of life, and that the pursuit of our dreams can lead to remarkable outcomes, no matter when we begin.These individuals, whether it's Julia Child finding her culinary passion in her 30s or Colonel Sanders building a global fast-food empire in his 60s, challenge the deeply ingrained societal belief that our most productive and fulfilling years are confined to youth. They prove that age is not a barrier to creativity, innovation, or personal growth.

Their stories are not isolated incidents; they represent a broader truth about human potential. They remind us that we are capable of remarkable feats at any stage of our lives. We can learn new skills, develop new passions, and achieve our dreams, regardless of our age or past experiences. These individuals serve as inspiring examples, demonstrating that the human spirit is inherently resilient and capable of adapting, evolving, and thriving throughout the entire lifespan. Their journeys encourage us to challenge the limitations imposed by societal expectations and embrace the possibilities that lie ahead, regardless of our age. They remind us that it's never too late to pursue our passions, to learn new things, and to make a meaningful contribution to the world. These stories are a powerful antidote to the narrative of decline, offering hope and inspiration to those who may feel that their time has passed. They demonstrate that the human spirit is capable of extraordinary things at any age, and that the pursuit of our dreams is a lifelong journey, filled with endless possibilities.

This book is divided into three parts. The first part, ***"The Spark Within,"*** explores the societal pressures and misconceptions surrounding age and achievement. It delves into the psychology behind these beliefs and challenges the notion that there is a "right" time to pursue our dreams. It also highlights the unique advantages that come with experience and maturity, demonstrating how these qualities can be powerful catalysts for success.

The second part, ***"Profiles in Perseverance,"*** forms the heart of the book. It features in-depth profiles of individuals who achieved extraordinary feats later in life. Each chapter tells the story of a different person, exploring their early life, the turning point that led them to pursue their later-life goals, the challenges they faced, and the ultimate triumph they achieved. These stories are not just biographical accounts; they are powerful narratives of resilience, determination, and the unwavering pursuit of passion.

The third part, ***"Igniting Your Own Potential,"*** is designed to empower readers to take action in their own lives. It provides practical exercises and strategies for identifying passions, overcoming obstacles, and taking the first steps towards achieving personal goals. It emphasizes the importance of self-belief, resilience, and the power of taking action, no matter how small.

"One Life, Never Too Late" is more than just a collection of inspiring stories. It's a call to action. It's an invitation to challenge the limiting beliefs that hold us back, to embrace the potential that lies within us, and to pursue our dreams with unwavering passion, regardless of our age. It's a reminder that life is not a race against the clock, but a journey of continuous growth, discovery, and possibility. It's a testament to the enduring truth: It's never too late.

PART ONE

The Spark Within

1
The Unexpected Bloom

"Age is an issue of mind over matter. If you don't mind, it doesn't matter."

- Mark Twain

The image is striking: a canvas bursting with vibrant colours, depicting a pastoral scene of rolling hills, quaint farmhouses, and figures engaged in everyday rural life. The artist, Anna Mary Robertson, better known as Grandma Moses, began painting in earnest in her late 70s, after arthritis made it too difficult for her to continue her previous pursuits of embroidery and farm work. With no formal training, she transformed her memories of rural life into captivating works of art, capturing the essence of a bygone era. Her paintings, filled with a childlike charm and a profound sense of nostalgia, resonated with audiences worldwide, making her a celebrated American folk artist. Grandma Moses's story is a powerful testament to the fact that creativity can blossom at any age, that talent can emerge from unexpected places, and that it is never too late to discover a hidden passion.

Grandma Moses isn't an isolated case. History is replete with examples of individuals who achieved remarkable feats later in life, defying societal expectations and proving that age is not a barrier to achievement. Consider Laura Ingalls Wilder, the beloved author of the "Little House on the Prairie" series. While she had written sporadically throughout her life, it wasn't until she was in her 60s that she began writing the books that would immortalize her family's pioneering experiences. Her stories, filled with vivid descriptions of frontier life and enduring themes of family and resilience, captivated generations of readers and cemented her place in literary history.

These stories, and countless others, challenge the pervasive narrative that our prime years are confined to youth and young adulthood. They shatter the myth that our potential diminishes with age, revealing the incredible capacity for growth, reinvention, and achievement that exists within each of us, regardless of our chronological age. They represent what we might call the "Unexpected Bloom" – the emergence of talent, passion, or purpose at a stage of life when society often expects us to be slowing down.

Why do we, as a society, so readily associate achievement, particularly groundbreaking achievement, with youth? This tendency is a complex issue with roots in various cultural and historical factors. One significant influence is the pervasive portrayal in media and popular culture of young people as the primary drivers of innovation, disruption, and future shaping. From Silicon Valley startups founded by young entrepreneurs to pop culture icons achieving fame in their teens and twenties, the narrative of youthful success is constantly reinforced. This constant exposure to stories of young achievers can create a skewed perception that equates youth with peak potential and innovation.

Another contributing factor is a deeply ingrained societal bias that equates aging with decline. This bias, often subtle and unconscious, assumes that our physical and mental capacities inevitably diminish over time. This assumption leads to the misconception that older individuals are less capable of learning new skills, adapting to change, or making significant contributions. This ageist perspective overlooks the wealth of experience, wisdom, and accumulated knowledge that comes with age. It focuses on perceived losses rather than recognizing the unique strengths and perspectives that older individuals bring.

Whatever the root cause, this narrow and limiting view of human potential has significant consequences, both for individuals and for society as a whole. For individuals, it can lead to self-doubt, a fear of pursuing new endeavours later in life, and a sense of resignation to a diminished future. It can prevent people from exploring their passions, developing their talents, and making meaningful contributions to their communities. For society as a whole, this ageist perspective results in a significant loss of potential and valuable contributions. By dismissing the capabilities of older individuals, we lose out on their wisdom, experience, and unique perspectives, hindering innovation and progress.

The reality is far more nuanced and complex than this simplified view of aging and achievement. Life is not a linear progression from a singular peak of performance to an inevitable decline. Instead, it's a dynamic and multifaceted journey, characterized by twists, turns, unexpected opportunities, and continuous growth. While it's undeniable that certain physical and cognitive changes occur as we age, these changes don't automatically translate to a loss of overall potential. In fact, for many people, the later years of life can be a period of profound growth, self-discovery, and remarkably fulfilling creative expression. This period can be a time for pursuing long-held dreams, developing new skills, and making significant contributions to society in ways that were not possible in earlier years. The accumulated wisdom, experience, and resilience gained over a lifetime can be powerful assets, providing a unique perspective and a deep understanding of the world. This understanding can then fuel creativity, innovation, and a renewed sense of purpose. The later years, freed from the pressures of career building and family raising, can offer the time, space, and perspective needed to pursue passions and make a lasting impact.

The Unexpected Bloom often arises from a confluence of factors, a unique intersection of personal readiness and external circumstances. While major life events like retirement, the loss of a loved one, or children leaving home can create the space for new pursuits, the spark can also ignite from within, through a gradual awakening, a slow but steady stirring of a long-dormant passion. This awakening might manifest as a persistent nagging feeling, a sense that something is missing, or a growing dissatisfaction with the status quo. It's not necessarily a sudden epiphany but rather a gradual increase in awareness, a slow burn that eventually ignites into a full-fledged flame.

This gradual awakening can be triggered by various experiences. It might be a chance encounter with a book, a film, a piece of music, or a conversation that suddenly resonates deeply, sparking a forgotten interest or revealing a hidden talent. It could be a period of introspection, a time of quiet reflection that allows long-buried desires to surface. Or it might be a gradual accumulation of small moments, seemingly insignificant experiences that collectively nudge an individual towards a new path.

For example, someone who always enjoyed writing as a child but pursued a practical career in business might find themselves increasingly drawn to creative writing workshops or online writing communities later in life. This growing interest could lead them to rediscover their passion for storytelling and eventually pursue a career as an author. Or someone who always had a fascination with astronomy but never had the opportunity to explore it might find themselves captivated by a documentary about space exploration, leading them to join an astronomy club and eventually pursue amateur astronomy or even astrophotography. These are not sudden transformations but rather the culmination of a gradual awakening, a slow but steady rediscovery of long-held passions.

Equally important is the role of circumstance, the unexpected opportunities that can present themselves at just the right moment. These opportunities might come in the form of a chance encounter, a new connection, a change in circumstances, or simply being in the right place at the right time. These moments of serendipity can provide the catalyst for the Unexpected Bloom, opening doors to new possibilities that might have otherwise remained hidden.

Consider the story of a woman who, after years of working as a stay-at-home mother, volunteers at a local animal shelter. This seemingly simple act of volunteering could lead her to discover a deep passion for animal welfare, leading her to pursue a career as a veterinarian technician or even start her own animal rescue organization. Or imagine a man who, after retiring from a career in engineering, takes a pottery class at a local community centre. This chance encounter with clay could ignite a hidden artistic talent, leading him to become a skilled potter and even open his own studio. These examples illustrate how unexpected circumstances can provide the spark for a new beginning, revealing hidden talents and passions that might have otherwise remained dormant.

It's crucial to understand that the gradual awakening and the role of circumstance are often intertwined. A gradual awakening might make someone more receptive to unexpected opportunities, while a chance encounter might accelerate a slow-burning passion. The Unexpected Bloom often arises from this dynamic interplay between inner readiness and external circumstances. It's about being open to new experiences, paying attention to the whispers of your inner voice, and recognizing the opportunities that life presents, even when they appear in unexpected forms. This combination of internal desire and external opportunity is often the fertile ground from which the most remarkable late-life achievements grow.

For Grandma Moses, it was the onset of arthritis that led her to pick up a paintbrush. Unable to continue her intricate embroidery work, she turned to painting as a new form of creative expression. What began as a simple pastime quickly blossomed into a full-fledged artistic career, bringing her international acclaim and solidifying her legacy as one of America's most beloved folk artists.

Laura Ingalls Wilder's path to literary success was also shaped by life's circumstances. Having experienced a life of hardship and constant moving on the American frontier, she began writing to preserve her memories for her daughter, Rose. These writings eventually evolved into the "Little House" series, capturing the hearts and imaginations of readers around the world.

These stories highlight a crucial point: the Unexpected Bloom is not about suddenly becoming a completely different person. It's about tapping into existing strengths, experiences, and passions in new and meaningful ways. It's about recognizing that our life experiences, both the triumphs and the challenges, have shaped us into the individuals we are today, providing a rich foundation for future growth and achievement.

The concept of the Unexpected Bloom offers a refreshing and liberating perspective on aging and human potential. It directly challenges the limiting narratives that equate aging with decline and instead encourages us to reconsider our deeply ingrained notions of what is possible at different stages of life. It urges us to look beyond the conventional timelines and societal expectations that often dictate when we should achieve certain milestones, such as career peaks, family building, or personal fulfillment. These timelines, often arbitrary and based on societal norms rather than individual realities, can create unnecessary pressure and a sense of inadequacy when individuals feel they are "falling behind" or not conforming to these pre-set paths.

The Unexpected Bloom invites us to embrace the possibility of discovering new passions, developing dormant talents, and achieving significant accomplishments at any age. It suggests that the potential for growth, learning, and creativity is not confined to youth but rather continues throughout our entire lifespan. It reframes aging not as a period of diminishing returns but as an opportunity for new beginnings, unexpected discoveries, and the realization of previously unforeseen potential. This concept is not about denying the natural changes that occur with age; it's about recognizing that these changes don't necessarily equate to a loss of capability or a decline in creativity. Instead, they can often provide a new lens through which to view the world, offering unique perspectives and insights that can fuel new passions and endeavours.

The Unexpected Bloom reminds us of several key truths about the human experience. First, it emphasizes the remarkable resilience of the human spirit. It highlights our innate capacity to adapt, overcome adversity, and find new purpose, even in the face of significant challenges or life changes. Second, it affirms that creativity is not a finite resource that diminishes with age; rather, it can flourish at any stage of life, often finding new and unexpected forms of expression. The accumulated wisdom, experience, and emotional depth that come with age can actually enrich creative output, providing a deeper well of inspiration and a more nuanced understanding of the human condition. Finally, and perhaps most importantly, the Unexpected Bloom reinforces the idea that it is truly never too late to begin again. It dismantles the myth of a limited window of opportunity, demonstrating that the pursuit of dreams, the development of new skills, and the achievement of significant goals are possible at any age.

This book will explore the lives of individuals who have experienced their own Unexpected Blooms, offering compelling real-life examples of late-life success and fulfillment. By delving into their stories, we will examine the various factors that contributed to their achievements, including their resilience, their willingness to embrace change, their supportive relationships, and their unwavering belief in themselves. We will extract key lessons from their experiences, providing practical insights and actionable strategies that we can all apply to our own lives. These stories will serve as a source of inspiration and encouragement, empowering readers to embrace their own potential for late-life growth and to pursue their passions with renewed vigour, regardless of their age or current circumstances.

2

The Time Trap

"The greatest mistake you can make in life is to be continually fearing you will make one."

- Elbert Hubbard

From the moment we enter formal education, we're placed on a conveyor belt of expectations. Graduate high school by eighteen, college by twenty-two, secure a stable job shortly thereafter, marry in your late twenties or early thirties, buy a house, start a family - these milestones are often presented as the natural, even inevitable, progression of a successful life. Society subtly, and sometimes not so subtly, reinforces these timelines, creating a sense of urgency, a feeling that we're constantly racing against the clock. This societal pressure to adhere to a pre-determined schedule creates what we can call "The Time Trap."

The Time Trap is the pervasive belief that there's a "right" time for everything, a narrow window of opportunity for achieving our goals. It's the feeling that if we haven't accomplished certain things by a certain age, we've somehow fallen behind, missed our chance. This can lead to feelings of anxiety, self-doubt, and even despair, as individuals compare themselves to others and worry that they're not "on track."

This pressure to conform to societal timelines is significantly amplified in the digital age, particularly by the pervasive influence of social media. Platforms like Instagram, Facebook, LinkedIn, and even TikTok have become virtual stages where individuals curate idealized versions of their lives, showcasing only the most polished and enviable moments. These carefully constructed narratives, often filtered and edited to perfection, create a distorted perception of reality, contributing significantly to the feeling of being "off track."

On social media, we are constantly bombarded with images of our peers achieving traditional milestones. We see engagement announcements with sparkling rings, wedding photos filled with joy and celebration, pictures of keys to new houses, and snapshots of smiling families with newborns. We witness career advancements, promotions, and awards, all presented as seamless triumphs. It's easy to scroll through these feeds and feel a pang of inadequacy if our own lives don't mirror these seemingly perfect trajectories.

This constant exposure to curated perfection creates a sense of social comparison, a phenomenon where individuals evaluate their own lives based on the perceived successes of others. This can lead to feelings of envy, self-doubt, and a sense of falling behind, even if our own lives are fulfilling and meaningful in their own way. We begin to measure ourselves against an unrealistic standard, a highlight reel that doesn't reflect the full spectrum of human experience.

The problem lies in the fact that social media often presents a highly selective and edited portrayal of reality. People rarely post about their struggles, their failures, or their moments of vulnerability. Instead, they showcase their best selves, their most successful moments, creating an illusion of effortless perfection. We rarely see the hard work, the setbacks, the anxieties, or the sacrifices that lie behind these carefully constructed narratives.

For example, a friend might post a picture of their new house, celebrating their achievement of homeownership. What we don't see are the years of saving, the stressful house-hunting process, the financial anxieties, or the countless hours spent on repairs and maintenance. Similarly, a colleague might announce a promotion on LinkedIn, but we don't see the long hours, the challenging projects, or the internal struggles they faced to reach that point.

This constant exposure to idealized versions of reality can be particularly damaging for those who are already feeling insecure or uncertain about their own path. It reinforces the Time Trap, making them feel like they're not keeping up with their peers and that they're somehow failing to meet societal expectations.

It's crucial to remember that social media is not an accurate reflection of reality. It's a carefully curated performance, a collection of highlights that doesn't tell the whole story. Everyone's journey is unique, and comparing ourselves to others based on their social media presence is inherently unfair and unproductive.

To break free from the Time Trap in the age of social media, we must cultivate a critical awareness of the content we consume. We need to remind ourselves that what we see online is not the full picture and that everyone's life is filled with both triumphs and challenges. We need to focus on our own journey, celebrating our own achievements, and defining success on our own terms, rather than comparing ourselves to the curated narratives of others. We must recognize that social media is a tool, and we have the power to control how it affects us. Choosing to focus on authentic connections and limiting exposure to idealized portrayals can be a crucial step in breaking free from the Time Trap and embracing our own unique path.

The Time Trap is particularly insidious because it's often internalized. We begin to police ourselves, setting arbitrary deadlines for our own achievements. We tell ourselves that we need to be a manager by thirty, own a house by thirty-five, have children by forty. These self-imposed limitations can be just as damaging as external pressures, preventing us from pursuing our passions or taking risks that could lead to greater fulfillment.

This societal obsession with timelines also creates a bias against those who deviate from the norm. Individuals who pursue education or career changes later in life, who choose not to marry or have children, or who simply take a different path are often viewed with suspicion or even judgment. They're seen as outliers, as somehow not conforming to the expected script.

The Time Trap doesn't just impose arbitrary timelines; it also perpetuates a deeply ingrained societal myth: that youth is synonymous with potential. This myth is constantly reinforced by media portrayals, popular culture, and even well-intentioned advice. We're bombarded with stories of young entrepreneurs who build billion-dollar companies in their early twenties, child prodigies who master complex skills at an astonishingly young age, and "overnight successes" who seemingly burst onto the scene with minimal effort. These narratives, while inspiring in some ways, can also create a distorted perception of achievement, suggesting that the prime years for innovation, creativity, and success are confined to youth and young adulthood.

This emphasis on youth can create a sense of urgency and anxiety, particularly for those who haven't achieved their desired level of success by a certain age. It reinforces the idea that if you haven't "made it" by your twenties or thirties, your best years are behind you, and your opportunities are dwindling. This can be profoundly discouraging for older individuals contemplating a career change, a new creative pursuit, or any form of self-reinvention. They may internalize these messages, believing they are "too old" to start something new, that they've missed their "window of opportunity," or that they lack the energy, adaptability, or cognitive capacity to compete with younger individuals.

This internalized ageism can be particularly damaging. It can lead to self-doubt, inaction, and a sense of resignation. Individuals may abandon their dreams before even attempting to pursue them, convinced that they are simply too late. They may tell themselves stories like, "I'm too old to go back to school," "I'm too old to start a business," or "I'm too old to learn a new skill." These limiting beliefs can prevent them from experiencing the joy, fulfillment, and potential that lie beyond their self-imposed barriers.

However, the stories of individuals who achieve remarkable feats later in life directly challenge this pervasive notion. They serve as powerful counter-narratives, demonstrating that the timeline we've been told to follow is not only arbitrary but also profoundly limiting and often inaccurate. These late bloomers prove that potential doesn't have an expiration date. They demonstrate that passion can ignite at any age, fueled by life experience, accumulated wisdom, and a renewed sense of purpose.

Consider the example of J.R.R. Tolkien, who published The Hobbit at the age of 45 and The Lord of the Rings trilogy between the ages of 62 and 71. Or consider the case of Morgan Freeman, who achieved widespread fame as an actor in his 50s and 60s, after decades of working in theatre and smaller film roles. These examples, and countless others, demonstrate that creative genius, career breakthroughs, and significant achievements can occur at any stage of life.

These stories prove that the pursuit of our dreams can lead to extraordinary outcomes, regardless of when we begin. They dismantle the myth that youth holds a monopoly on potential, demonstrating that experience, resilience, and a deep understanding of oneself can be just as valuable, if not more so, in the pursuit of meaningful goals. They offer hope and inspiration to anyone who feels they've missed their chance, reminding us that it's never too late to ignite our passions and make our mark on the world. They show that while youth may have its own advantages, the later stages of life bring their own unique strengths, creating a different but equally potent kind of potential waiting to be unleashed.

Breaking free from the constricting grip of the Time Trap demands a fundamental shift in perspective, a conscious rejection of the pervasive notion that there exists a singular "right" way to live or a rigid, predetermined timeline for achieving success. This shift necessitates embracing the inherent diversity of human experience and acknowledging the profound truth that every individual's journey is unique, unfolding at its own pace and according to its own rhythm. It's about recognizing that there is no universal template for a successful life, no one-size-fits-all approach to happiness or fulfillment.

The Time Trap perpetuates the harmful myth that there is a "correct" sequence for life events–education, career, marriage, family–and that deviating from this prescribed order constitutes failure or falling behind. This creates immense pressure to conform, leading to feelings of anxiety, inadequacy, and self-doubt when individuals find themselves on a different path. However, by embracing the diversity of human experience, we recognize that there are countless valid ways to live a fulfilling life. Some may choose to prioritize career advancement in their 20s, while others may discover their passion later in life. Some may choose to marry and have children early, while others may choose a different path. There is no single "right" answer, and embracing this diversity allows us to liberate ourselves from the pressure to conform.

This liberation also requires us to critically examine and challenge our own internalized beliefs about age and potential. The Time Trap operates not only through external societal pressures but also through deeply ingrained internal narratives. These narratives, often unconsciously absorbed from family, culture, and media, dictate what we believe is possible for us at different stages of life. They whisper insidious messages about being "too old" to start something new, "too late" to pursue a dream, or "past our prime" for achieving significant success.

Dismantling these internalized beliefs is a crucial step in breaking free from the Time Trap. It requires a conscious effort to identify and challenge these negative self-perceptions. We must question the validity of these limiting beliefs and recognize that they are often based on outdated assumptions and societal stereotypes rather than objective reality. This process of challenging internalized beliefs begins with becoming aware of the negative thoughts and self-limiting beliefs you hold about age and potential. Pay attention to the internal dialogue and identify recurring themes of self-doubt or age-related limitations. Once you've identified these beliefs, challenge the evidence supporting them. Are these beliefs based on facts or assumptions? Are they based on your own experiences or on societal stereotypes? Often, these beliefs crumble under scrutiny when examined objectively. Then, actively replace negative self-talk with positive affirmations and more realistic perspectives. Instead of thinking "I'm too old to learn this new skill," try reframing it as "I have valuable life experience that can help me learn this skill in a unique way." It is also helpful to remind yourself of your strengths, your past accomplishments, and the skills you have already acquired. This helps to build confidence and counteract negative self-perceptions. Release the pressure of adhering to arbitrary deadlines. Recognize that there is no set timeline for achieving your goals and that it's never too late to begin.

Ultimately, breaking free from the Time Trap requires a fundamental shift in how we value ourselves. We need to recognize that our worth and potential are not tied to our age, our accomplishments, or external validation, but to our inherent worth as human beings. This intrinsic value remains constant throughout our lives, regardless of our age or achievements. By embracing this truth, we can liberate ourselves from the pressure to conform to external expectations and embrace the unique unfolding of our own individual journeys. We can begin to see aging not as a period of decline but as a period of continued growth, learning, and self-discovery, a time to pursue passions, embrace new challenges, and live a life filled with purpose and meaning, regardless of the number of years we have lived. This recognition of inherent worth is the key that unlocks the door to a life lived free from the constraints of the Time Trap.

By dismantling the Time Trap, by dismantling the deeply ingrained belief that there's a single "right" time for everything, we unlock a world of previously unimaginable possibilities. We unshackle ourselves from the self-imposed limitations and societal expectations that have confined us, opening ourselves up to a life of greater freedom, purpose, and fulfillment. This liberation allows us to pursue our passions with renewed vigor, to embrace calculated risks without the paralyzing fear of "being too late," and to recognize and seize the unexpected opportunities that life inevitably presents along the way. It's about shifting from a mindset of scarcity and limitation to one of abundance and possibility, recognizing that the potential for growth and achievement is not confined to a specific age or stage of life.

This dismantling of the Time Trap creates the fertile ground for what we've termed the "Unexpected Bloom." This concept refers to the emergence of talents, passions, or a renewed sense of purpose later in life, often in ways that were previously unforeseen. It's about recognizing that our potential is not a static entity but a dynamic force that can manifest in surprising and wonderful ways throughout our lifespan. By freeing ourselves from the constraints of the Time Trap, we create the space for this Unexpected Bloom to occur, allowing our hidden talents and long-dormant passions to finally surface and flourish, regardless of our age. This is not about denying the realities of aging, but rather about recognizing that aging itself can be a catalyst for new beginnings and unexpected discoveries.

When we are no longer bound by the pressure to conform to a pre-determined timeline, we become more open to exploring new interests, developing new skills, and pursuing new ventures. We are no longer limited by the fear of "falling behind" or "missing our chance." This newfound freedom allows us to take risks that we might have previously avoided, to step outside our comfort zones, and to embrace the unknown with greater confidence and enthusiasm. It's about shifting from a mindset of "I should have done this earlier" to one of "I'm doing this now, and I'm excited to see where it leads."

This shift in perspective also allows us to recognize and seize unexpected opportunities. When we are not fixated on a rigid plan or timeline, we become more attuned to the subtle cues and serendipitous encounters that life presents. We are more likely to recognize and capitalize on these opportunities, even if they deviate from our original plans. This openness to the unexpected can lead to surprising and rewarding outcomes, opening doors to new paths and enriching our lives in profound ways.

The following chapters in Part II will delve into the lives of individuals who have successfully broken free from the constraints of the Time Trap. These are not exceptional cases or isolated incidents; they are real-life examples of ordinary people who have dared to defy societal expectations and pursue their dreams at various stages of life. Their stories will illuminate the incredible power of pursuing one's passions, regardless of the perceived timeline. They will demonstrate that age is not a barrier to achievement, that potential does not diminish with time, and that the human spirit is capable of remarkable resilience, creativity, and growth throughout the entire lifespan. These narratives will provide inspiration, encouragement, and practical insights for anyone seeking to break free from the Time Trap and embrace the full potential of their own unique journey. They will show us that it is never too late to begin, to grow, to create, and to live a life filled with purpose and passion.

3
The Advantage of Experience

"The older I get, the more I realize the importance of all the experiences, the good and the bad, everything has made me who I am today."

- C.S. Lewis

While societal pressures often emphasize the perceived advantages of youth, the reality is that growing older brings a wealth of unique strengths and perspectives that can be powerful catalysts for achievement. The often-overlooked advantages of experience, demonstrating how accumulated wisdom, resilience, and a deeper understanding of oneself can pave the way for extraordinary accomplishments later in life.

One of the most significant advantages of experience is the accumulation of wisdom. Over time, we gather a vast storehouse of knowledge, not just from formal education or training, but also from navigating the complexities of life. We learn from our successes and, perhaps even more importantly, from our failures. We develop a nuanced understanding of human nature, of the world around us, and of our own strengths and weaknesses. This accumulated wisdom provides a valuable foundation for making informed decisions, overcoming challenges, and pursuing our goals with greater clarity and purpose.

This wisdom often manifests as a greater sense of perspective. As we age, we tend to develop a broader view of life, recognizing that setbacks are temporary and that challenges can be opportunities for growth. We become less prone to impulsive reactions and more capable of making thoughtful, considered choices. This perspective can be particularly valuable when pursuing long-term goals, providing the resilience and patience needed to navigate obstacles and stay focused on the ultimate objective.

One of the most significant benefits of navigating the complexities of a long life is the development of resilience. Life, with its inherent unpredictability, inevitably presents us with challenges, setbacks, and moments of profound adversity. These "curveballs," as they are often called, can manifest in various forms, from personal losses and career disappointments to financial struggles and health issues. While such experiences can be deeply painful and difficult to endure, they also serve as invaluable opportunities for growth, forging within us a strength and adaptability that is crucial for achieving later-life goals. Resilience, therefore, is not about avoiding hardship; it's about developing the capacity to bounce back from it, to learn from our mistakes, and to emerge stronger and more determined.

With each setback we overcome, we build greater emotional strength, a deeper understanding of our own capabilities, and a more nuanced perspective on life's inherent fluctuations. This accumulated experience becomes a reservoir of inner strength, providing the fortitude to persevere through future difficulties and remain committed to our vision, especially when pursuing ambitious goals later in life. This isn't a passive process; resilience is an active practice of learning and adaptation, a continuous cycle of facing adversity, processing its impact, and finding ways to move forward.

This process of building resilience involves several key components, each contributing to our ability to weather life's storms: acceptance, learning from mistakes, maintaining perspective, seeking support, and focusing on solutions. Acceptance involves recognizing and acknowledging the reality of a difficult situation, rather than denying or resisting it. This allows us to avoid getting bogged down in unproductive emotions and instead focus our energy on finding constructive solutions. Learning from mistakes is equally crucial. By analyzing what went wrong, identifying areas for improvement, and using these experiences to refine our approach, we transform setbacks into valuable lessons. This process of self-reflection and adaptation is essential for growth and development.

Maintaining perspective is another vital component of resilience. It involves recognizing that setbacks are temporary and that they do not define our worth or our potential. This broader perspective helps us avoid getting discouraged by temporary setbacks and allows us to maintain a positive outlook, even in the face of adversity. Seeking support from others, whether it's family, friends, mentors, or support groups, provides emotional comfort, practical assistance, and a sense of belonging. Sharing our burdens with others can lighten the load and provide valuable insights and perspectives. Finally, focusing on solutions is essential for moving forward. It involves shifting our focus from dwelling on the problem to actively seeking ways to overcome the obstacle and find a path forward.

The individuals profiled in this book exemplify the power of resilience in action. Diana Nyad's relentless pursuit of the Cuba-Florida swim is a prime example. She faced multiple failed attempts, enduring physical exhaustion, debilitating jellyfish stings, and challenging ocean currents. Each setback could have been a reason to abandon her dream, but Nyad used these experiences as opportunities to learn, adapt, and strengthen her resolve. She refined her strategy, improved her equipment, and honed her mental fortitude. Her ultimate success at the age of 64 is a powerful testament to the transformative power of resilience.

Similarly, Colonel Sanders' story illustrates the importance of resilience in the face of financial hardship. He faced financial ruin in his 60s when a new highway bypassed his restaurant, drastically reducing his business. This devastating setback could have easily led him to despair and resignation. However, he refused to be defeated. He embarked on a tireless journey to franchise his chicken recipe, facing numerous rejections and setbacks along the way. His unwavering persistence and resilience ultimately led to the creation of a global fast-food empire, a remarkable achievement born from the ashes of adversity.

These examples demonstrate that resilience is not an innate trait reserved for a select few; it's a skill that is developed and honed through experience. The challenges we face throughout our lives, while often painful and unwelcome, provide us with the invaluable opportunity to cultivate this essential quality. This accumulated resilience becomes an invaluable asset when pursuing ambitious goals, especially later in life, providing the fortitude to persevere through difficulties and remain committed to our vision.

This resilience is particularly crucial for those embarking on new endeavours later in life. They may encounter unique challenges, such as ageism, physical limitations, or a perceived lack of experience in a new field. However, their accumulated life experience has equipped them with the resilience to navigate these obstacles and pursue their goals with unwavering determination. They have learned from past setbacks, developed coping mechanisms, and gained a deeper understanding of their own strengths and weaknesses. This hard-earned resilience becomes a powerful catalyst for late-life achievement, transforming potential roadblocks into stepping stones on the path to success. It allows them to not just survive adversity but to thrive because of it, viewing setbacks not as endings but as detours on the journey to achieving their dreams.

In essence, experience provides a unique advantage: the ability to navigate the inevitable challenges of life with greater strength, wisdom, and perspective. This resilience becomes a cornerstone for pursuing ambitious goals at any age, but especially later in life, when the accumulation of life experience provides a wellspring of inner strength to draw upon.

A significant advantage that comes with accumulated life experience is the development of a clearer, more nuanced understanding of oneself. As we navigate the complexities of life, encountering diverse situations, building relationships, and facing both triumphs and setbacks, we gain invaluable insights into our own values, passions, and priorities. We become more attuned to the subtle nuances of our strengths and weaknesses, allowing us to make choices that resonate more deeply with our authentic selves. This self-knowledge, often a gradual and ongoing process, becomes a powerful compass, guiding us toward paths that are truly aligned with our inner compass. This is especially important when pursuing new endeavours later in life, providing the clarity and focus needed to pursue goals that are not merely externally driven but intrinsically meaningful and fulfilling.

This clearer sense of self is not simply an intellectual understanding; it's a deep, embodied knowing that comes from lived experience. It's about understanding what truly motivates us, what brings us joy, and what we value most in life. This self-awareness allows us to make choices that are congruent with our authentic selves, leading to a greater sense of purpose and fulfillment. It also allows us to avoid pursuing goals that are based on external pressures or societal expectations, leading to a more authentic and satisfying life path. This enhanced self-understanding brings several key benefits. It provides greater clarity of purpose; when we understand our values and priorities, we gain a clearer sense of direction in life. We are better able to identify goals that are truly meaningful to us and to prioritize our time and energy accordingly. Self-knowledge also allows for more informed decision-making. We are better able to assess our strengths and weaknesses, to evaluate opportunities based on their alignment with our values, and to make choices that are in our best interests. Furthermore, when we are grounded in a strong sense of self, we are better equipped to handle challenges and setbacks, demonstrating increased resilience. We are less likely to be swayed by external criticism or self-doubt, and we are more likely to persevere in the face of adversity. Finally, self-awareness also improves our relationships with others. When we understand ourselves better, we are better able to communicate our needs and boundaries, to build stronger connections, and to navigate interpersonal challenges more effectively.

This clearer sense of self often leads to greater confidence. Having navigated various life experiences, both positive and negative, we develop a stronger sense of self-assuredness and a greater belief in our own abilities. We have faced challenges, overcome obstacles, and learned from our mistakes, building a reservoir of experience that reinforces our belief in our capacity to handle whatever comes our way. This confidence is not arrogance or bravado; it's a quiet inner knowing that we have the resources and resilience to navigate life's complexities. This confidence acts as a powerful motivator, empowering us to take risks, embrace challenges, and pursue our goals with greater conviction. When we believe in ourselves, we are more likely to step outside our comfort zones, to try new things, and to persevere in the face of difficulties. This self-belief fuels our determination and allows us to overcome obstacles that might have previously seemed insurmountable. This increased confidence manifests in several ways. It leads to a greater willingness to take risks; when we believe in ourselves, we are less afraid of failure and more willing to take calculated risks. We understand that failure is a part of the learning process and that even setbacks can provide valuable lessons. Confidence also provides increased resilience in the face of challenges. We are less likely to be discouraged by setbacks and more likely to bounce back stronger and more determined. Furthermore, when we are confident in our abilities, we are more likely to assert ourselves and pursue our goals with conviction, demonstrating greater assertiveness in pursuing goals. We are less likely to be swayed by external pressures or self-doubt. Finally, confidence enhances our communication skills and strengthens our relationships with others, leading to improved communication and relationships. We are better able to express our needs and boundaries, to communicate effectively, and to build strong, meaningful connections.

This combination of self-knowledge and confidence creates a powerful synergy, empowering individuals to pursue their passions and achieve their full potential, especially later in life. This inner strength, born from years of experience and self-discovery, allows them to approach new endeavours with greater clarity, purpose, and conviction, transforming the later years into a period of profound growth, fulfillment, and meaningful contribution.

Intelligence and Age

In the realm of cognitive abilities, understanding the distinction between fluid and crystallized intelligence is crucial for appreciating the cognitive strengths that develop with age. Fluid intelligence refers to the capacity to think quickly and reason abstractly, to solve novel problems and adapt to new situations. It involves working memory, processing speed, and the ability to identify patterns and relationships. This type of intelligence tends to peak in young adulthood and may gradually decline with age. Crystallized intelligence, conversely, represents the accumulation of knowledge, skills, and experience gained throughout life. It encompasses accumulated facts, vocabulary, general knowledge, and expertise in specific domains. Unlike fluid intelligence, crystallized intelligence continues to grow and expand throughout adulthood, becoming a significant asset as we age.

This distinction is essential because it challenges the simplistic notion that all cognitive abilities decline with age. While some aspects of fluid intelligence may change, crystallized intelligence provides a rich storehouse of information and insights that can be applied to new situations, challenges, and learning experiences. This accumulated knowledge base allows older adults to draw upon a vast network of connections and experiences, enabling them to approach problems with a broader perspective and a deeper understanding.

How does growth of crystallized intelligence help us.

Enhanced Problem-Solving

Accumulated knowledge and experience provide a broader context for understanding problems and identifying potential solutions. Older adults can draw upon a larger repertoire of past experiences to inform their decision-making, often leading to more effective and nuanced solutions.

Improved Decision-Making

Crystallized intelligence contributes to better judgment and decision-making by providing a deeper understanding of cause-and-effect relationships, potential consequences, and the complexities of human behaviour.

Greater Expertise

Through years of experience and learning, individuals develop expertise in specific domains. This expertise can be invaluable in professional settings, creative endeavours, and personal pursuits.

Enhanced Communication Skills

Vocabulary and language skills, key components of crystallized intelligence, continue to develop throughout life. This can lead to improved communication skills, both written and verbal.

Increased Wisdom and Insight

The combination of accumulated knowledge and life experience contributes to greater wisdom and insight. Older adults are often able to see the bigger picture, to understand complex situations, and to offer valuable advice and guidance.

This distinction between fluid and crystallized intelligence highlights a crucial point: while some cognitive abilities may change with age, others continue to develop and strengthen. The wisdom, perspective, resilience, self-knowledge, and, importantly, crystallized intelligence that come with experience can be incredibly valuable assets in the pursuit of later-life achievements. These qualities provide a unique advantage, allowing older adults to approach new challenges with a wealth of resources that younger individuals may not yet possess. They are not starting from scratch; they are building upon a foundation of accumulated knowledge and experience, allowing them to make significant contributions in various fields.

This understanding of crystallized intelligence also has implications for how we approach learning and development in later life. It suggests that focusing on activities that leverage existing knowledge and skills, while also providing opportunities to learn new information and expand one's knowledge base, can be particularly beneficial. Activities such as reading, writing, engaging in discussions, pursuing hobbies, and learning new skills can all contribute to the continued growth of crystallized intelligence and enhance cognitive function in later years. It's a reminder that learning is a lifelong process and that the capacity for intellectual growth and development continues throughout our lives.

The advantages of experience are evident in the stories of many individuals who achieved remarkable feats later in life. Ray Kroc, for example, didn't find success with McDonald's until his 50s. His previous experiences in sales and marketing, combined with his unwavering persistence and clear vision, provided the foundation for building a global fast-food empire. Diana Nyad's successful swim from Cuba to Florida at the age of 64 was the culmination of decades of training, setbacks, and unwavering determination. Her accumulated experience and resilience were crucial to her ultimate triumph.

These stories demonstrate that while youth may bring certain advantages, experience offers a unique set of strengths that can be equally, if not more, valuable in the pursuit of our goals. The wisdom, perspective, resilience, self-knowledge, and crystallized intelligence that come with age can provide a powerful foundation for achieving extraordinary things, proving that it's never too late to pursue our passions and make our mark on the world. This understanding is crucial for breaking free from the Time Trap and embracing the possibility of the Unexpected Bloom. The following chapters will delve into the lives of individuals who have harnessed the power of their experience to achieve remarkable feats, providing inspiring examples of what is possible when we embrace the advantages of growing older.

PART TWO

Profiles in Perseverance

4

Ray Kroc - The Hamburger Hustler

"Luck is a dividend of sweat. The more you sweat, the luckier you get."

- Ray Kroc

Ray Kroc's story is a quintessential American tale of late-blooming success. He wasn't a young, tech-savvy entrepreneur disrupting an industry from his garage. He was a 52-year-old milkshake machine salesman, a man who had spent decades navigating the world of sales and marketing, searching for that elusive "big break." He found it not in a ground breaking invention or a revolutionary technology, but in a humble hamburger stand in San Bernardino, California. The story of Ray Kroc and McDonald's is a testament to the power of vision, persistence, and the ability to recognize opportunity where others see only the ordinary.

Born in 1902 in Oak Park, Illinois, Raymond Albert Kroc's early life was marked by a restless spirit and a series of diverse experiences. He wasn't a stellar student, dropping out of high school to serve as an ambulance driver during World War I, although the war ended before he could be deployed overseas. Upon his return, he dabbled in various jobs, from playing piano to selling paper cups. These early experiences, while seemingly disparate, instilled in him a strong work ethic and a deep understanding of the art of salesmanship.

For much of his adult life, Kroc worked as a multi-mixer milkshake machine salesman. He travelled extensively, pitching his machines to soda fountains and restaurants across the country. This experience provided him with valuable insights into the food service industry, exposing him to different business models and customer preferences. It was during one of these sales trips, in 1954, that he encountered the McDonald brothers' restaurant.

Dick and Mac McDonald had revolutionized the fast-food industry with their "Speedee Service System," a streamlined operation that focused on efficiency and consistency. They offered a limited menu of high-quality hamburgers, french fries, and milkshakes, prepared and served with remarkable speed. Kroc was immediately impressed. He recognized the potential of their system, not just as a single restaurant, but as a nationwide chain.

At the time, the McDonald brothers were content with their small, successful operation. They had franchised a few locations, but their focus was on maintaining quality and control, not rapid expansion. Kroc, however, saw a much grander vision. He envisioned a network of McDonald's restaurants spanning the country, offering the same consistent quality and experience to customers everywhere. He saw an opportunity to build an empire.

Kroc's initial proposal to the McDonald brothers was to become their franchising agent. He convinced them that he could expand their brand far beyond their current reach. In 1955, at the age of 52, he founded McDonald's System, Inc. (later McDonald's Corporation), and began his quest to build a fast-food empire.

The early years were far from easy. Kroc faced numerous challenges, including securing financing, finding suitable locations, and maintaining consistency across the growing number of franchises. He often clashed with the

McDonald brothers, who were more concerned with preserving their original methods than embracing rapid expansion. They were resistant to many of Kroc's ideas, preferring to keep the business small and manageable.

One of Kroc's key innovations was his meticulous attention to detail and standardization. He understood that consistency was crucial to building a successful brand. He developed detailed operating manuals that outlined every aspect of the McDonald's system, from the precise weight of the hamburger patties to the exact temperature of the french fry oil. He established Hamburger University in Elk Grove Village, Illinois, to train franchisees in his methods, ensuring that every McDonald's restaurant delivered the same quality and experience to customers.

Ray Kroc's vision for McDonald's transcended the simple act of selling hamburgers; he possessed a keen understanding of the broader business landscape and recognized the critical role of strategic planning in achieving long-term success. A key element of his vision, and arguably one of the most significant factors in McDonald's enduring dominance, was his strategic focus on real estate. Kroc understood that location was paramount in the restaurant business, but his vision extended beyond simply finding good locations; he implemented a strategy of purchasing the land on which McDonald's restaurants were built. This seemingly simple decision had profound implications for the company's future.

By purchasing the land, Kroc secured a significant advantage over other franchise models. Instead of simply leasing properties, McDonald's owned the underlying real estate, giving the company far greater control over its operations. This ownership provided stability, eliminating the risk of lease renewals, rent increases, or landlords deciding to repurpose the property. It also provided a valuable asset base. As real estate values appreciated over time, these land holdings became a substantial source of wealth for the company, contributing significantly to its financial strength and long-term stability. This strategic foresight transformed McDonald's from a mere restaurant chain into a major real estate holder, creating a dual revenue stream and solidifying its financial foundation.

This real estate strategy had several key benefits. It provided greater control over the restaurant's operations, allowing the company to make necessary renovations, expansions, or other modifications without needing landlord approval. It also allowed them to control the surrounding environment to some extent, ensuring that neighbouring businesses were compatible with the McDonald's brand and customer experience. This control extended to parking, signage, and other factors that contributed to the overall customer experience. Owning the land also provided a significant financial advantage. As property values increased, the company's assets grew substantially, creating a valuable financial cushion and providing access to capital for further expansion. This real estate portfolio also provided a hedge against inflation, as real estate values tend to rise with inflation, protecting the company's investments.

Furthermore, this strategy created a powerful incentive for franchisees. By leasing the land to franchisees, McDonald's generated a steady stream of rental income. This provided a consistent revenue source for the company, even during economic downturns. It also created a strong alignment of interests between the company and its franchisees. Franchisees were invested in the success of their individual restaurants, while the company benefited from the overall growth of the franchise system and the appreciation of its real estate assets. This symbiotic relationship proved to be a powerful engine for growth.

Kroc's emphasis on real estate was not merely a tactical decision; it was a strategic vision that fundamentally shaped the trajectory of McDonald's. It transformed the company from a regional hamburger stand into a global powerhouse, not just in the fast-food industry but also in the world of commercial real estate. This strategic foresight, this ability to see beyond the immediate product and understand the broader business context, was a key factor in Kroc's success and continues to be a defining characteristic of McDonald's long-term strategy. It exemplifies the importance of looking beyond the immediate transaction and considering the long-term implications of business decisions, particularly in the realm of asset management and strategic planning.

Despite his initial agreement with the McDonald brothers, Kroc's vision for the company diverged significantly from theirs. They were focused on maintaining control and preserving their original concept, while Kroc was driven by ambition and a desire for rapid expansion. This led to increasing tensions between them.

In 1961, Kroc finally bought out the McDonald brothers for $2.7 million, a significant sum at the time. This acquisition gave him complete control of the company and allowed him to fully realize his vision. He continued to expand the franchise network, implementing innovative marketing strategies and adapting the menu to changing consumer preferences.

Kroc's relentless pursuit of growth and his unwavering belief in the McDonald's system transformed the company into a global phenomenon. By the time of his death in 1984, McDonald's had become the largest fast-food chain in the world, a testament to his vision, persistence, and business acumen.

Ray Kroc's story offers several valuable lessons for aspiring entrepreneurs and anyone pursuing their goals later in life. Kroc possessed a clear vision of what McDonald's could become, even when others saw only a small hamburger stand. This vision provided the driving force behind his relentless pursuit of growth. Kroc faced numerous obstacles and setbacks throughout his journey, but he never gave up on his vision. His persistence and determination were crucial to his ultimate success. While Kroc was committed to maintaining consistency in the McDonald's system, he was also willing to adapt to changing market conditions and consumer preferences. This adaptability allowed the company to remain relevant and competitive over time. Kroc saw potential in the McDonald brothers' system where others saw only the ordinary. His ability to recognize and capitalize on this opportunity was the catalyst for his extraordinary success. Kroc's meticulous attention to detail and his emphasis on standardization were crucial to maintaining consistency and quality across the growing franchise network. This focus on systems became a cornerstone of McDonald's success.

Ray Kroc's story is a powerful reminder that it's never too late to pursue your dreams. He found his greatest success in his 50s, proving that age is not a barrier to achievement. His journey is an inspiration to anyone who feels they've missed their "window of opportunity," demonstrating that with vision, persistence, and a willingness to adapt, extraordinary things can be achieved at any stage of life. He transformed a local hamburger joint into a global empire, leaving a lasting legacy on the world of business and proving that the Unexpected Bloom can lead to remarkable results.

5

Diana Nyad: The Relentless Swimmer

"Never, ever give up. You're never too old to chase your dreams."

- Diana Nyad

Diana Nyad's name is synonymous with perseverance, a testament to the unwavering human spirit's ability to overcome seemingly insurmountable obstacles. Her relentless pursuit of a seemingly impossible dream - swimming from Cuba to Florida without a shark cage - captivated the world, not just for the sheer athletic feat it represented, but for the powerful message it conveyed: it's never too late to chase your dreams, no matter how audacious they may seem.

Born in 1949 in New York City, Diana Nyad's early life was marked by a strong connection to the water. She began swimming at a young age and quickly demonstrated a natural talent for the sport. Her early swimming career was promising, but she eventually transitioned to long-distance swimming, a discipline that would define her life and legacy.

In 1978, at the age of 28, Nyad made her first attempt to swim from Cuba to Florida. This grueling 103-mile journey across the treacherous Florida Straits presented a multitude of challenges: strong currents, unpredictable weather, the threat of sharks, and the sheer physical and mental endurance required to spend over two days in the open ocean. After 42 hours in the water, battling strong currents and rough seas, Nyad was forced to abandon her attempt.

This setback, however, did not deter her. Nyad's spirit remained unbroken, and the dream of conquering the Florida Straits continued to burn within her. She went on to achieve other remarkable feats in long-distance swimming, including swimming around Manhattan Island in 1975 and swimming from the Bahamas to Florida in 1979. But the Cuba-Florida swim remained her ultimate goal, a challenge that she felt compelled to conquer.

For over three decades, Nyad put her Cuba-Florida dream on hold, focusing on other pursuits, including journalism and motivational speaking. But the dream never truly faded. In her 60s, a time when many people are considering slowing down, Nyad felt a renewed sense of purpose, a powerful urge to return to the water and finally achieve her long-held ambition.

In 2011, at the age of 61, Nyad embarked on her second attempt to swim from Cuba to Florida. This time, she was better prepared, with improved equipment, including a specially designed shark-repelling suit and a support team that was meticulously trained to handle every possible contingency. However, even with these advancements, the challenge remained immense. After 29 hours in the water, she was forced to stop due to severe jellyfish stings and strong currents.

Undeterred, Nyad attempted the swim again in 2012, at the age of 62. This attempt was also thwarted by jellyfish stings and rough seas. Many would have considered these repeated failures as a sign to give up, to accept that the dream was simply too difficult to achieve. But Diana Nyad was not one to be easily discouraged. Her resilience, her unwavering belief in her own abilities, and her deep-seated desire to conquer this challenge fueled her determination to try again.

In 2013, at the age of 64, Diana Nyad made her fifth and final attempt to swim from Cuba to Florida. This time, everything aligned. The weather conditions were favourable, the currents were manageable, and her support team was perfectly synchronized. After 52 hours, 54 minutes, and 18.6 seconds of relentless swimming, Diana Nyad stepped onto the shore of Key West, Florida, becoming the first person to successfully swim from Cuba to Florida without a shark cage.

This achievement was not just a personal triumph for Nyad; it was a powerful symbol of human resilience and the limitless potential of the human spirit. It demonstrated that age is not a barrier to achieving extraordinary things, that dreams can be pursued and conquered at any stage of life.

Nyad's journey offers several invaluable lessons. Nyad faced numerous setbacks and failures throughout her pursuit of the Cuba-Florida swim, but she never gave up. Her resilience, her ability to bounce back from adversity, was crucial to her ultimate success. Nyad's unwavering determination to achieve her dream fueled her through years of training, setbacks, and doubt. Her commitment to her goal was unwavering, even when faced with seemingly insurmountable obstacles. Nyad's dream of swimming from Cuba to Florida was considered by many to be impossible. But she refused to accept limitations, believing that with enough preparation, determination, and support, anything was possible.While Nyad's determination and resilience were essential, her success was also due to meticulous preparation. She trained rigorously for years, refining her technique, building her endurance, and assembling a highly skilled support team. Nyad's support team played a crucial role in her success. They provided her with encouragement, logistical support, and medical assistance throughout her journey. Their dedication and expertise were essential to her achievement.

Nyad's story is particularly inspiring because she achieved her goal later in life, proving that age is not a deterrent to pursuing ambitious dreams. In a society that often emphasizes youth and discounts the potential of older individuals, Nyad's achievement stands as a powerful counter-narrative. She demonstrated that experience, wisdom, and a deep understanding of oneself can be powerful assets in the pursuit of extraordinary goals.

Diana Nyad's historic swim from Cuba to Florida is far more than a mere athletic accomplishment; it transcends the realm of sports and becomes a potent metaphor for the human journey itself. It serves as a powerful reminder that life is not a sprint, a frantic dash to a finish line, but rather a marathon, a long and arduous journey filled with its share of challenges, setbacks, and, ultimately, moments of hard-won triumph. Nyad's relentless pursuit, spanning decades and culminating in her successful crossing at the age of 64, is a testament to the enduring power of the human spirit to overcome adversity and achieve what many deem impossible. Her story resonates deeply because it mirrors the struggles and triumphs that we all experience in our own lives, albeit on a different scale.

Nyad's journey to conquer the Florida Straits was not a smooth, uninterrupted path. It was marked by multiple failed attempts, each one presenting its own unique set of obstacles. She faced the physical challenges of extreme endurance, battling fatigue, dehydration, and hypothermia. She endured the constant threat of marine life, including painful jellyfish stings and the ever-present danger of sharks. She wrestled with the unpredictable forces of nature, contending with strong currents, choppy seas, and adverse weather conditions. Each of these setbacks could have been a reason to give up, a justification for abandoning her seemingly impossible dream. Yet, with each failure, Nyad returned to the water, more determined than ever, learning from her mistakes, refining her strategy, and strengthening her resolve. This unwavering persistence, this refusal to surrender in the face of adversity, is at the heart of her story's power.

Her swim becomes a metaphor for the challenges we all face in life, whether they are professional setbacks, personal losses, health issues, or any other form of adversity. Like Nyad facing the vast expanse of the ocean, we often encounter obstacles that seem insurmountable. We may experience moments of doubt, fear, and even despair. But Nyad's story reminds us that even in the face of these challenges, the human spirit possesses an extraordinary capacity for resilience. It reminds us that we have the inner strength to persevere, to adapt, and to overcome even the most daunting obstacles.

Nyad's achievement is also a beacon of hope and inspiration, particularly for those who feel they have missed their chance or that their dreams are no longer attainable. Her success at the age of 64 challenges the societal narrative that achievement is primarily a domain of the young. It proves that it's never too late to chase your dreams, no matter how audacious they may seem. It dismantles the myth of a limited window of opportunity, demonstrating that passion, determination, and hard work can lead to extraordinary outcomes at any age. It sends a powerful message that age is not a barrier to achieving one's full potential; rather, it can be a source of strength, wisdom, and resilience.

Her relentless pursuit of her dream embodies the very spirit of this book–the idea that one life, lived with purpose and passion, is indeed never too late. Nyad's journey is not just about swimming; it's about the human capacity for growth, resilience, and the unwavering pursuit of meaning. It's about finding one's passion, setting ambitious goals, and refusing to give up, even when faced with seemingly insurmountable obstacles. It's about recognizing that the journey itself, with all its challenges and triumphs, is what truly matters. It is a powerful reminder that the potential for growth, discovery, and achievement is a lifelong journey, a marathon of the human spirit, and that one life, lived with purpose and passion, is indeed never too late.

6

Harland Sanders: The Colonel's Secret Recipe

"I made my mistakes, but I didn't let them stop me. I just kept going."

- Colonel Sanders

Colonel Harland Sanders, the iconic face of Kentucky Fried Chicken, is a prime example of someone who found extraordinary success later in life. His story isn't one of overnight fame or instant riches. It's a tale of perseverance, resilience, and unwavering belief in his product, even in the face of numerous setbacks and disappointments. It's a powerful reminder that it's never too late to pursue your dreams and that even after decades of struggle, success can still be within reach.

Born in 1890 in Henryville, Indiana, Harland David Sanders' early life was marked by hardship. His father died when he was just six years old, forcing his mother to work to support the family. This early loss placed a significant burden on young Harland, who took on various responsibilities, including cooking for his younger siblings. This early experience in the kitchen would unknowingly lay the foundation for his future culinary success.

Sanders left home at the age of 13 and embarked on a series of diverse jobs, reflecting a restless spirit and a desire to find his place in the world. He worked as a farmhand, a railroad fireman, a steamboat pilot, an insurance salesman, and even a blacksmith's helper. These varied experiences, while seemingly unrelated, instilled in him a strong work ethic, a resourcefulness, and a deep understanding of human nature.

In his 40s, Sanders took over a motel and began serving food to travellers. It was here, in Corbin, Kentucky, that he perfected his now-famous fried chicken recipe, using a pressure cooker to speed up the cooking process and a secret blend of 11 herbs and spices to create a unique and flavourful product. His restaurant quickly gained popularity, attracting travellers and locals alike.

Sanders' restaurant became a popular stop for those passing through Corbin, particularly during the Great Depression. He earned a reputation for his delicious fried chicken and his warm hospitality. In 1935, Kentucky Governor Ruby Laffoon bestowed upon him the honorary title of "Kentucky Colonel" in recognition of his contributions to the state's cuisine. This title would become synonymous with his name and his brand.

However, just as Sanders was enjoying success, disaster struck. In the 1950s, a new interstate highway was built, bypassing Corbin and significantly reducing traffic to his restaurant. This sudden downturn in business forced him to sell his restaurant at a loss. At the age of 65, Sanders found himself with little more than a Social Security check and his secret chicken recipe.

This could have been the end of the story. Many would have considered retirement at this stage of life, accepting the setback as a sign to give up. But Harland Sanders was not one to be easily discouraged. He believed in his product, he believed in his recipe, and he believed that he still had something to offer the world.

Instead of succumbing to despair, Sanders embarked on a new venture: franchising his fried chicken recipe. He travelled across the country, visiting restaurants and offering to share his recipe in exchange for a small royalty on each chicken sold. This process was far from easy. He faced numerous rejections and encountered many skeptical restaurant owners.

But Sanders' persistence and unwavering belief in his product eventually paid off. He secured his first franchise in Salt Lake City, Utah, in 1952. From there, the Kentucky Fried Chicken franchise network began to grow, slowly at first, but then with increasing momentum.

Colonel Harland Sanders, the founder of Kentucky Fried Chicken, was not just a purveyor of delicious fried chicken; he was a master of branding and a charismatic personality who became synonymous with his product. His distinctive appearance—the iconic white suit, the crisp black string tie, and the neatly trimmed white goatee—became an integral and instantly recognizable part of the brand's image. This carefully cultivated persona was not accidental; it was a deliberate strategy that played a crucial role in building Kentucky Fried Chicken into a household name.

Sanders understood the power of visual branding long before it became a mainstream marketing concept. His white suit, reminiscent of a Southern gentleman or a riverboat gambler, conveyed an image of trustworthiness, quality, and old-fashioned hospitality. It set him apart from other fast-food entrepreneurs and created a memorable visual identity for the brand. The string tie and goatee further enhanced this image, adding a touch of folksy charm and down-home authenticity. This carefully crafted image wasn't just for show; it reflected Sanders' own personality and values, making him a genuine and relatable figure to the public.

Beyond his appearance, Sanders actively promoted his chicken, becoming the face of the brand. He understood that personal connection was vital in building trust and loyalty with customers. He appeared in countless commercials, often delivering folksy anecdotes and homespun wisdom along with his endorsements of the chicken. These commercials weren't slick, high-budget productions; they were simple, direct, and focused on Sanders' personality and the quality of his product. This approach resonated with audiences who were tired of overly polished advertising and appreciated Sanders' genuine and relatable persona.

Sanders also made numerous public appearances, visiting restaurants, attending events, and interacting directly with customers. He was a natural showman, with a warm personality and a knack for storytelling. His folksy charm and down-to-earth demeanour endeared him to people from all walks of life. This direct interaction with the public helped to build a strong emotional connection between the brand and its customers. People didn't just feel like they were buying fried chicken; they felt like they were buying a piece of Colonel Sanders' story and his unique brand of Southern hospitality.

This combination of a distinctive visual image and a charismatic personality proved to be a powerful marketing strategy. Sanders became more than just a founder; he became a cultural icon, a symbol of quality, and the living embodiment of the Kentucky Fried Chicken brand. His image was used on packaging, signage, and advertising materials, further solidifying his connection to the product. This consistent branding helped to create a strong and recognizable identity for the company, making it stand out in a crowded marketplace.

Sanders' impact on the Kentucky Fried Chicken brand is undeniable. His distinctive appearance, active promotion, and warm personality were instrumental in transforming a small roadside restaurant into a global fast-food empire. He understood that building a successful brand was about more than just selling a product; it was about creating a connection with customers, building trust, and telling a compelling story. His legacy continues to influence the brand today, serving as a reminder of the power of personality, authenticity, and a well-crafted image in building a lasting brand identity.

By the mid-1960s, Kentucky Fried Chicken had become a nationwide phenomenon, with hundreds of franchises across the United States. In 1964, at the age of 74, Sanders sold his interest in the company for $2 million (equivalent to roughly $18 million today). However, he remained the face of the brand, continuing to appear in commercials and promoting the chicken that he had perfected over decades.

The story of Colonel Sanders offers several key lessons:

- **Persistence** Sanders faced numerous setbacks throughout his life, including the loss of his restaurant in his 60s. But he never gave up on his dream, demonstrating the power of persistence in achieving long-term goals.

- **Belief in Your Product** Sanders had unwavering confidence in his fried chicken recipe. This belief fueled his determination to franchise his product, even when faced with rejections and skepticism.

- **Adaptability** While Sanders was committed to his original recipe, he was also willing to adapt to changing market conditions and consumer preferences. This adaptability was crucial to the growth and success of the Kentucky Fried Chicken brand.

- **Branding and Marketing** Sanders understood the importance of creating a strong brand identity. His distinctive appearance and warm personality became an integral part of the Kentucky Fried Chicken brand, helping to connect with customers on a personal level.

- **It's Never Too Late** Sanders achieved his greatest success later in life, proving that age is not a barrier to achieving extraordinary things. His story is an inspiration to anyone who feels they've missed their "window of opportunity."

Colonel Harland Sanders' life story stands as a powerful and enduring testament to the fact that success can be found, and indeed often blossoms, at any age. His journey defies the conventional narrative of youthful achievement, demonstrating that the later years of life can be a time of remarkable accomplishment and profound impact. Sanders didn't achieve widespread recognition or build his global empire until his 60s and 70s, a period when many consider retirement a foregone conclusion. His late-life success powerfully illustrates that experience, resilience, and an unwavering belief in one's product or vision can lead to extraordinary outcomes, even after decades of struggle, setbacks, and relative obscurity.

Sanders' early life was marked by hardship and a series of diverse occupations, none of which brought him significant financial success or widespread recognition. He worked as a farmhand, a railroad fireman, an insurance salesman, and a ferryboat operator, among other jobs. He faced numerous business failures and personal setbacks, including the loss of his father at a young age and various financial difficulties. These early struggles, however, were not simply a prelude to failure; they were the crucible in which his resilience, determination, and resourcefulness were forged. They provided him with a wealth of life experience, an understanding of human nature, and a deep appreciation for the value of hard work.

It was in his 40s that Sanders began serving his now-famous fried chicken at a roadside motel in Corbin, Kentucky. Over the next two decades, he perfected his "secret recipe" of 11 herbs and spices and developed a unique pressure-frying method that produced consistently delicious and crispy chicken. However, a significant turning point came in his 60s when a new interstate highway bypassed his restaurant, drastically reducing his business and forcing him to sell it. Facing financial ruin at an age when many would have given up, Sanders embarked on a tireless journey to franchise his chicken recipe. He traveled across the country, often sleeping in his car, visiting restaurants, and pitching his idea to potential franchisees. He faced countless rejections, enduring numerous disappointments and setbacks. Yet, he never wavered in his belief in the quality of his product and the potential for his business to succeed.

It was this unwavering belief, coupled with his resilience and accumulated experience, that ultimately led to his remarkable success. By the time he was in his 70s, Kentucky Fried Chicken had become a rapidly growing franchise, and Sanders had become a recognizable and beloved figure. He transformed a simple fried chicken recipe, born out of necessity and refined through years of experimentation, into a global fast-food empire, solidifying his place not only in culinary history but also in the annals of business achievement.

Sanders' journey embodies the very spirit of this book—the powerful message that one life, lived with purpose, passion, and unwavering determination, is indeed never too late to achieve one's dreams and leave a lasting impact on the world. His story is a powerful reminder that age is not a barrier to success, that experience can be a valuable asset, and that perseverance can transform even the most challenging circumstances into opportunities for extraordinary achievement. He serves as an inspiration to anyone who feels they have missed their chance or that their dreams are no longer attainable, demonstrating that with passion, resilience, and an unwavering belief in oneself, it is indeed never too late to create a legacy.

7

Grandma Moses - The Accidental Artist

"Life is what we make it, always has been, always will be."

- Grandma Moses

Anna Mary Robertson, better known to the world as Grandma Moses, is a captivating example of how talent can emerge from the most unexpected places and at the most unexpected times. Her story isn't one of a lifelong dedication to art or formal training at prestigious academies. It's a story of a woman who, in her late 70s, discovered a passion and a talent that would transform her life and leave an indelible mark on the art world. Grandma Moses's journey is a powerful testament to the fact that creativity can blossom at any age and that it's never too late to discover a hidden passion.

Born on a farm in Greenwich, New York, in 1860, Anna Mary Robertson's early life was deeply rooted in rural America. She grew up working on the family farm, attending a one-room schoolhouse, and experiencing the rhythms of rural life. Her formal education was limited, but she possessed a keen observation of the world around her, a deep appreciation for nature, and a strong connection to her rural heritage.

At the age of 12, she left home to work as a hired girl on a neighbouring farm. This experience, while demanding, further ingrained in her a strong work ethic and a deep understanding of farm life, which would later become a central theme in her artwork. In 1887, she married Thomas Moses, a farmer, and they moved to a farm in Virginia. They later returned to New York State, settling in Eagle Bridge.

For much of her life, Anna Mary Moses focused on the practicalities of farm life and raising her five children. She was known for her domestic skills, particularly her embroidery and needlework. These creative pursuits, while not considered "high art," nurtured her artistic sensibilities and honed her eye for colour and design.

It was in her late 70s, after her husband's death and as arthritis made needlework increasingly difficult, that Anna Mary Moses turned to painting. She had always enjoyed creating, and with her previous creative outlet becoming challenging, she sought a new form of expression. She began painting scenes of rural life, drawing inspiration from her childhood memories and her deep connection to the land.

With no formal training, Grandma Moses painted with a directness and simplicity that became her signature style. Her paintings, often described as "primitive" or "folk art," depicted scenes of everyday life in rural America: farm work, harvest festivals, winter landscapes, and children playing. Her use of vibrant colours, her attention to detail, and her ability to capture the essence of rural life resonated with viewers, evoking a sense of nostalgia and a connection to a simpler time.

Initially, Grandma Moses's paintings were sold at local fairs and exhibitions. Her work caught the attention of a local collector, Louis Caldor, who recognized her unique talent and began promoting her work. In 1939, her paintings were included in an exhibition at the Museum of Modern Art in New York City, although they were displayed anonymously as part of a folk art exhibition.

Her career truly took off in 1940 when her work was featured in a solo exhibition at a New York City gallery. This exhibition brought her widespread recognition and launched her into the national spotlight. Suddenly, this elderly woman from rural New York became a celebrated artist, her paintings sought after by collectors and museums alike.

Grandma Moses's artistic career, which began in her late 70s, experienced a remarkable surge in popularity throughout the 1940s and 1950s, solidifying her status as a beloved American folk artist. Her charming depictions of rural life, with their vibrant colours and nostalgic scenes, resonated deeply with a public yearning for simpler times. This widespread appeal propelled her work beyond the confines of art galleries and into the mainstream of American culture.

A key factor in Grandma Moses's growing fame was the widespread reproduction of her paintings on various commercial products. Her artwork began appearing on greeting cards, calendars, and other merchandise, making her art accessible to a much broader audience than traditional art exhibitions could reach. This widespread distribution exposed her work to millions of people who might not have otherwise encountered it, further cementing her place in popular culture. These reproductions not only disseminated her art but also contributed to her growing fame, making her name and her distinctive style instantly recognizable.

The commercial success of her work on merchandise was not merely a matter of chance; it was a testament to the broad appeal of her art. Her paintings evoked a sense of nostalgia for a simpler, more rural past, a theme that resonated strongly with many Americans, particularly during and after World War II. Her work offered a comforting and idealized vision of rural life, providing a sense of escape from the anxieties and complexities of modern life. This broad appeal translated into strong sales of her reproduced artwork, further fuelling her fame and recognition.

As her popularity grew, Grandma Moses received numerous awards and accolades, further validating her artistic talent and solidifying her position as a prominent figure in the art world. These honours not only recognized her artistic achievements but also celebrated her as a symbol of perseverance, creativity, and the potential for late-life achievement. Among these prestigious awards were the Women's National Press Club trophy, which she received in 1949. This national recognition further cemented her status as a prominent figure in American culture. In 1951, she was honored with the New York State's "Woman of the Year" award, a testament to her significant contributions to the art world and her inspiring story of late-life success.

These accolades, combined with the widespread distribution of her work on merchandise, propelled Grandma Moses to national and even international fame. She became a cultural icon, a symbol of the enduring power of creativity and the potential for personal fulfillment at any age. Her story became an inspiration to countless individuals, demonstrating that it's never too late to pursue one's passions and make a meaningful contribution to the world. Her art, once a personal pastime, became a source of joy and inspiration for millions, solidifying her legacy as one of America's most beloved folk artists.

Despite her late start, Grandma Moses enjoyed a remarkably prolific career. She continued to paint well into her 90s, producing over 1,600 paintings. Her work is now held in the collections of major museums around the world, including the Metropolitan Museum of Art, the Museum of Modern Art, and the National Gallery of Art.

Grandma Moses's story offers several important lessons:

- **Creativity Can Emerge at Any Age** Grandma Moses began painting in her late 70s, proving that creativity is not limited by age. Her story is an inspiration to anyone who feels they've missed their chance to pursue a creative passion.

- **Embrace New Beginnings** When arthritis made needlework difficult, Grandma Moses embraced painting as a new form of creative expression. Her willingness to adapt and explore new avenues led to her remarkable success.

- **Trust Your Instincts** Grandma Moses had no formal training, yet she trusted her instincts and painted in a style that was uniquely her own. Her directness and simplicity became her signature, resonating with viewers around the world.

- **Find Inspiration in Your Experiences** Grandma Moses drew inspiration from her childhood memories and her deep connection to rural life. Her paintings captured the essence of a bygone era, connecting with viewers on an emotional level.

- **The Importance of Recognition and Support** The recognition and support that Grandma Moses received from collectors and galleries played a crucial role in her success. This highlights the importance of fostering a supportive environment for artists of all ages.

Grandma Moses's story is a powerful example of the Unexpected Bloom. She discovered her true calling later in life, proving that talent can emerge from unexpected places and at unexpected times. Her journey is an inspiration to anyone who feels they have a hidden passion waiting to be discovered. She transformed her memories of rural life into captivating works of art, leaving a lasting legacy on the art world and proving that one life is indeed never too late to find your true calling. Her “accidental” entry into the art world became a celebrated career, inspiring countless individuals to pursue their passions, regardless of age.

8

Stan Lee - The Man Behind the Masks

"With great power comes great responsibility."

- Stan Lee

Stan Lee, the iconic figurehead of Marvel Comics, wasn't just a comic book writer and editor; he was a storyteller, a visionary, and a cultural icon. While he had a long and productive career in the comic book industry, his greatest influence and widespread recognition came later in life, particularly with the rise of Marvel's cinematic universe in the 21st century. His story is a powerful illustration of how creativity can endure and thrive over decades, and how the seeds planted early in a career can blossom into extraordinary success later in life.

Born Stanley Martin Lieber in 1922 in New York City, Stan Lee's early life was marked by a love for reading and storytelling. During the Great Depression, his family struggled financially, and young Stan sought refuge in books and movies, developing a vivid imagination and a passion for creating his own stories.

In 1939, at the age of 17, Lee landed a job as an office assistant at Timely Comics, a pulp magazine publisher that would later become Marvel Comics. His initial tasks were menial – filling inkwells, fetching lunch, and proofreading. However, he quickly demonstrated a talent for writing, and soon he was writing text fillers and eventually full comic book stories.

His first published work was a text filler titled "Case of the Curious Crime of the Costume," which appeared in Captain America Comics #3 in 1941. Shortly thereafter, he co-created his first superhero, the Destroyer. In 1942, at the age of 19, Lee became interim editor at Timely Comics, a position he would hold for many years.

During the 1940s and 1950s, Lee wrote and edited numerous comics, working in various genres, including romance, westerns, horror, and humor. The comic book industry experienced periods of boom and bust during this time, and Lee adapted to the changing trends, honing his skills as a writer and storyteller.

A pivotal moment that dramatically altered the course of Stan Lee's career, and indeed the trajectory of the entire comic book industry, arrived in the early 1960s. The comic book landscape at that time was facing a significant downturn in sales, and the superhero genre, once a dominant force, was widely perceived to be fading into obsolescence. The prevailing trend in comics had shifted away from superheroes, and the characters that remained were often seen as simplistic, one-dimensional, and out of touch with the changing cultural landscape. These characters were typically portrayed as paragons of virtue, possessing superhuman abilities and unwavering moral compasses, with little in the way of relatable human flaws or internal struggles.

It was during this period of industry decline that Lee, then working as an editor and writer at Marvel Comics (then known as Timely Comics), found himself at a creative crossroads. He was contemplating leaving the comic book industry altogether, feeling creatively stifled by the limitations of the existing superhero narratives. However, a crucial intervention came from his wife, Joan Lee. She encouraged him to take a risk, to try something different, to create the kind of stories he himself would want to read, even if it meant potentially losing his job. She urged him to stop trying to cater to perceived market demands and instead focus on creating characters that were more authentic and relatable.

This encouragement proved to be the catalyst for a creative revolution. Lee decided to break away from the established conventions of the superhero genre and introduce a new breed of characters. He envisioned superheroes that were not perfect, infallible beings but rather complex individuals with relatable human flaws, internal conflicts, and personal struggles. He wanted to create characters that readers could connect with on an emotional level, characters who reflected the anxieties, insecurities, and everyday challenges of ordinary people.

This shift in approach was a radical departure from the prevailing trend. Instead of portraying superheroes as untouchable icons, Lee sought to humanize them, giving them relatable problems like financial difficulties, relationship issues, and self-doubt. These characters were not immune to the challenges of everyday life; they grappled with moral dilemmas, made mistakes, and experienced genuine emotional turmoil. This humanization of superheroes was a groundbreaking concept that resonated deeply with readers.

This decision to create more relatable and flawed superheroes marked a turning point not only for Lee's career but for the entire comic book industry. It ushered in what is now known as the "Marvel Age of Comics," a period of unprecedented creativity and innovation that revitalized the genre and introduced some of the most iconic and enduring characters in popular culture. This willingness to take a risk, to defy conventional wisdom, and to focus on creating authentic and relatable characters transformed the landscape of comics and cemented Stan Lee's legacy as one of the most influential figures in the history of the medium.

In collaboration with artists like Jack Kirby and Steve Ditko, Lee co-created some of the most iconic superheroes of all time: the Fantastic Four, Spider-Man, the Hulk, Thor, Iron Man, the X-Men, and many others. These characters were groundbreaking in their complexity and relatability. They had personal problems, insecurities, and flaws, making them more appealing to readers who could see themselves reflected in these fantastical figures.

Lee's writing style was also innovative. He used a more conversational and engaging tone, addressing readers directly and creating a sense of community among comic book fans. He also introduced the concept of the "Marvel Universe," a shared continuity where characters from different titles could interact and cross over into each other's stories, creating a richer and more immersive reading experience.

The Marvel Comics of the 1960s became a cultural phenomenon, attracting a new generation of readers who were drawn to the characters' relatable struggles and the imaginative stories. Lee's role as writer, editor, and tireless promoter of Marvel Comics earned him a devoted following and established him as a major figure in the comic book industry.

Despite the significant success Stan Lee achieved during the 1960s, a period now known as the "Marvel Age of Comics," his influence and recognition experienced an even more dramatic surge in the later decades of his life, particularly with the advent and explosive growth of Marvel's cinematic universe in the 21st century. While his comic book creations had already left an indelible mark on popular culture, the transition of these characters to the big screen amplified their reach exponentially, introducing them to a global audience of millions who had never before encountered them within the pages of a comic book.

The 21st century witnessed a seismic shift in the entertainment landscape, with superhero films becoming a dominant force in Hollywood and global box offices. This phenomenon, largely fuelled by the success of Marvel Studios' interconnected cinematic universe, brought Lee's creations to life in a way that had never been possible before. Movies like "Spider-Man," "Iron Man," "The Avengers," "X-Men," "Thor," "Captain America," and countless others became cultural touchstones, captivating audiences of all ages and backgrounds. These films were not simply adaptations of comic book stories; they were meticulously crafted cinematic experiences that captured the essence of Lee's characters, their human flaws, their heroic struggles, and their enduring appeal.

This cinematic explosion had a profound impact on Lee's legacy. While he was already revered within the comic book community, the movies propelled him to international superstardom. He became a beloved figure to a new generation of fans who knew him primarily as the affable cameo performer in Marvel films. His signature catchphrases, his infectious enthusiasm, and his genuine love for his creations resonated with audiences worldwide. These brief but memorable appearances in the films cemented his image as the "face of Marvel," further solidifying his iconic status. The movies brought increased visibility and recognition, introducing Lee and his creations to a vastly larger audience than comic books alone could ever reach. This global exposure elevated him to the status of a pop culture icon, recognized and celebrated by millions around the world. The cinematic success of his characters served as a powerful validation of Lee's creative vision, demonstrating the enduring appeal of his humanized superheroes and the timeless quality of his storytelling. The movies ensured that Lee's creations would continue to be enjoyed and appreciated by future generations, providing a lasting testament to his contributions to popular culture and ensuring that his characters would remain relevant and influential for years to come. The immense commercial success of the MCU also brought Lee significant financial rewards, allowing him to enjoy the fruits of his creative labour in his later years.

The rise of the MCU transformed Stan Lee from a comic book legend into a global phenomenon. It brought his characters to life in a spectacular way, introducing them to millions who had never experienced the magic of Marvel comics. This cinematic success not only cemented his legacy but also amplified his influence on popular culture, ensuring that his creations would continue to inspire and entertain audiences for generations to come. It was a fitting culmination to a remarkable career, solidifying his place as one of the most influential figures in the history of comics and popular culture.

Lee became a beloved figure in popular culture, making cameo appearances in nearly every Marvel movie, often delivering humorous lines or offering sage advice. His enthusiasm for the characters and his genuine connection with fans made him a beloved figure at comic book conventions and other public events.

Stan Lee's story offers several important lessons:

- **Creativity Can Endure and Evolve** Lee's career spanned decades, during which he constantly adapted to changing trends and found new ways to express his creativity. His ability to evolve and innovate was crucial to his long-term success.

- **Collaboration is Key** Lee's collaborations with artists like Jack Kirby and Steve Ditko were essential to the creation of Marvel's iconic characters. He understood the power of teamwork and recognized the importance of bringing together different talents and perspectives.

- **Relatability is Powerful** Lee's decision to create flawed and relatable superheroes was a key factor in Marvel's success. He understood that readers connected more deeply with characters who faced real-world problems and struggles.

- **Embrace New Platforms** Lee embraced new media and technologies, recognizing the potential of movies, television, and the internet to reach a wider audience. His willingness to adapt to the changing media landscape contributed significantly to Marvel's global success.

- **The Power of Passion** Lee's lifelong passion for storytelling and his genuine enthusiasm for his characters were contagious. His passion resonated with fans and helped to build a strong community around Marvel Comics.

Stan Lee's career trajectory offers a compelling illustration of the idea that the seeds of success, planted early in one's career, can blossom into extraordinary achievements decades later. While he dedicated a significant portion of his life to the comic book industry, building a solid foundation and creating a vast array of beloved characters, his greatest influence and widespread recognition arrived later in life, coinciding with the meteoric rise of Marvel's cinematic universe (MCU). This phenomenon brought his creations to a global audience, catapulting him to international fame and solidifying his legacy as a pop culture icon.

Lee's early career in comics, spanning several decades, was marked by both creative triumphs and periods of relative obscurity. He worked tirelessly as a writer, editor, and publisher, contributing significantly to the development of the comic book medium. However, it wasn't until the 21st century, with the advent of big-budget superhero films, that his work reached its widest audience and garnered him the widespread recognition he deserved. This demonstrates that even if initial efforts don't immediately translate into widespread fame or fortune, the groundwork laid during those early years can be crucial for future success. It's a testament to the power of perseverance, dedication, and the importance of continuing to hone one's craft, even when immediate rewards are not apparent.

The success of the MCU served as a powerful amplifier for Lee's creative legacy. The films brought his characters to life in a way that had never been possible before, introducing them to millions who had never read a comic book. This global exposure transformed Lee from a respected figure within the comic book community into a household name, recognized and celebrated by audiences worldwide. This late-life surge in popularity underscores the idea that creativity is not confined to a specific age or stage of life; it can endure and thrive over time, finding new avenues for expression and reaching new audiences in unexpected ways.

Lee's story is a powerful reminder that one life is indeed never too late to achieve lasting impact. His influence on popular culture, particularly through the MCU, is undeniable. His characters, with their relatable human flaws and inspiring heroic qualities, have resonated with generations of readers and viewers, shaping the cultural landscape in profound ways. This lasting impact, achieved largely in the later decades of his life, serves as an inspiration to anyone who feels they have missed their chance or that their dreams are no longer attainable. It demonstrates that the potential for creativity, innovation, and meaningful contribution can continue to grow and evolve throughout one's lifespan.

His story also highlights the importance of adaptability and embracing new opportunities. Lee was willing to embrace the new medium of film and to collaborate with a new generation of filmmakers, allowing his creations to reach a wider audience. This openness to change and willingness to adapt to new technologies and platforms was crucial to his late-life success. It's a valuable lesson for anyone seeking to pursue their passions later in life: be open to new possibilities, embrace change, and don't be afraid to explore uncharted territory.

"Excelsior!" as he would say. This signature catchphrase, meaning "ever upward," perfectly encapsulates the spirit of his life and career. It embodies the idea of continuous striving, constant improvement, and the unwavering pursuit of excellence. It's a fitting epitaph for a man who continued to inspire and entertain audiences throughout his life, demonstrating that one life, lived with passion, creativity, and a relentless pursuit of one's vision, is indeed never too late to achieve lasting impact.

9

Fauja Singh : The Turbaned Tornado

"Age is just a number."

- Fauja Singh

Fauja Singh's story is not just about running marathons; it's a testament to the indomitable human spirit, a powerful narrative of resilience, and a vibrant illustration of how finding purpose later in life can lead to extraordinary achievements. He didn't begin running until his late 80s, a time when many people are slowing down, yet he went on to become the oldest person to ever complete a marathon, earning the moniker "The Turbaned Tornado." His journey is an inspiring reminder that age is just a number and that it's never too late to discover new passions and push the boundaries of what's considered possible.

Born in India in 1911, Fauja Singh's early life was far from that of a future marathon runner. He had weak legs and struggled to walk properly as a child, earning him the nickname "danda," meaning "stick," a reference to his thin limbs. He spent much of his youth working on his family's farm, his physical limitations preventing him from engaging in strenuous activities.

For decades, Singh lived a quiet life as a farmer, raising a family and tending to his land. He didn't participate in any organized sports or physical activities. Running was not even a remote consideration. He lived a simple life, focused on his family and his work.

The turning point in Singh's life came much later, in the 1990s, when he experienced a series of devastating personal losses. His wife passed away, and shortly thereafter, he lost one of his sons. These profound losses left him deeply grief-stricken and searching for a way to cope with his pain.

In his late 80s, seeking solace and a new purpose, Singh turned to running. It wasn't a planned decision to become a marathon runner; it was a desperate attempt to find an outlet for his grief and improve his overall well-being. He began running short distances near his home in England, where he had moved to be with his other children.

Initially, running was a struggle. His body was not accustomed to the physical exertion, and he faced numerous challenges, including aches, pains, and the simple difficulty of putting one foot in front of the other. But Singh persevered, driven by an inner strength and a desire to overcome his grief.

He soon connected with Harmander Singh, a running coach who would play a crucial role in his journey. Harmander Singh recognized Fauja Singh's determination and potential and began training him systematically. He adapted training methods to suit Singh's age and physical condition, focusing on building endurance and preventing injuries.

The training was rigorous, involving long runs, strength training, and careful attention to diet and rest. Singh faced numerous obstacles, not only due to his advanced age but also due to the sheer physical demands of marathon training. However, he approached each challenge with unwavering dedication and a positive attitude.

As Singh's fitness improved, he began participating in local races and gradually increased the distances he was running. He completed his first marathon at the age of 89, an already remarkable achievement. But this was just the beginning.

Singh's story began to attract media attention, and he became an inspiration to people around the world. His remarkable achievements challenged conventional notions about aging and demonstrated the incredible capacity of the human body and mind to adapt and overcome limitations.

In 2011, at the age of 100, Fauja Singh achieved what many considered impossible: he completed the Toronto Waterfront Marathon, becoming the oldest person to ever officially finish a marathon. His time was 8 hours, 25 minutes, and 16 seconds. While his time was not competitive with younger runners, the fact that he completed the 26.2-mile distance at his age was a monumental accomplishment.

This achievement garnered worldwide media attention, cementing Singh's status as a global icon of resilience and determination. He became a symbol of hope and inspiration, proving that it's never too late to pursue your dreams, regardless of age or physical limitations.

Even after his record-breaking marathon, Singh continued to run, participating in shorter races and inspiring others to embrace an active lifestyle. He became an advocate for healthy aging and encouraged people of all ages to pursue their passions.

Fauja Singh's story offers several valuable lessons:

- **Resilience in the Face of Adversity** Singh faced significant personal losses and physical challenges, but he never allowed these obstacles to define him.

His resilience and ability to bounce back from adversity were crucial to his success.

- **Finding Purpose in Later Life** Singh found a new purpose in running after experiencing personal tragedies. This demonstrates the importance of finding meaning and fulfillment at every stage of life.

- **The Power of Positive Thinking** Singh maintained a positive attitude throughout his training and racing, even when faced with difficulties. This positive mindset played a significant role in his ability to overcome challenges.

- **The Importance of Community and Support** Singh's coach, Harmander Singh, and his support team played a crucial role in his success. They provided him with guidance, encouragement, and practical assistance.

- **Challenging Age Stereotypes** Singh's achievements shattered conventional notions about aging and demonstrated that age is not a barrier to achieving extraordinary things. He inspired countless individuals to challenge their own perceived limitations.

- **The Importance of Physical Activity for Well-being** Singh's story highlights the benefits of physical activity for both physical and mental health, particularly in later life.

Fauja Singh's life story is a powerful testament to the idea that it is never too late to discover one's passion and ignite the inner fire that drives us to pursue our dreams. He didn't begin running until his late 80s, an age when many people are slowing down and focusing on rest. Yet, he defied all expectations, embarking on a remarkable journey that transformed him into a world-renowned marathon runner, inspiring millions across the globe with his extraordinary achievements. His story transcends the realm of athletics; it becomes a symbol of human potential, resilience, and the power of the human spirit to overcome perceived limitations.

Singh's decision to start running at such an advanced age was motivated by personal loss and a desire to find solace and purpose. After the death of his wife, he sought an outlet for his grief and a way to maintain his physical and mental well-being. Running became that outlet, a way to channel his emotions and rediscover a sense of purpose. This late-life discovery of running was not a carefully calculated career move; it was a deeply personal journey of healing and self-discovery.

His transformation from a non-runner in his late 80s to a marathon runner in his 90s is nothing short of extraordinary. He faced numerous challenges, including the physical demands of training at an advanced age, the skepticism of others, and the inevitable aches and pains that come with long-distance running. Yet, he persevered, driven by an inner determination and a newfound passion for running. He trained diligently, gradually increasing his distance and building his endurance. He embraced the challenges, viewing them not as obstacles but as opportunities to push himself further and prove what was possible.

Singh's achievements in the world of marathon running are remarkable. He completed multiple marathons, including the Toronto Waterfront Marathon at the age of 100, becoming the oldest person ever to complete a marathon. His accomplishments garnered international attention, making him a media sensation and an inspiration to people of all ages. His story resonated with millions because it challenged conventional notions of aging and demonstrated that physical and mental capabilities can be maintained and even enhanced well into old age.

His journey embodies the very spirit of this book–the central message that one life is indeed never too late to discover new possibilities and achieve extraordinary things. Singh's story is not just about running marathons; it's about the human capacity for reinvention, the power of resilience, and the unwavering pursuit of personal goals, regardless of age or circumstance. He shows us that the desire for growth, the pursuit of passion, and the ability to achieve extraordinary things are not limited by age or societal expectations.

He literally ran his way into history, becoming a symbol of hope and inspiration for people of all ages. His story transcends cultural and generational boundaries, reminding us that the human spirit is capable of remarkable feats when fueled by passion, purpose, and unwavering determination. He demonstrated that even at 100, an age typically associated with decline and limitations, one can still chase their dreams, push their boundaries, and achieve what many would consider impossible. Fauja Singh's life is a powerful reminder that it's never too late to find your fire and live a life filled with purpose, passion, and extraordinary achievements.

10

Jessica Tandy : A Timeless Performance

"Life begins at the end of your comfort zone."

- Neale Donald Walsch

Jessica Tandy's story is a compelling narrative of perseverance, dedication to craft, and a testament to the fact that recognition and acclaim can arrive at any stage of a career. While she had a long and respected career on the stage, it was her later-life performance in the film *Driving Miss Daisy* that propelled her to international stardom and solidified her place in cinematic history. Her journey is a powerful reminder that talent endures, and that the spotlight can shine brightly even after decades of dedicated work.

Born in London, England, in 1909, Jessica Alice Tandy demonstrated an early interest in acting. She received training at the Ben Greet Academy of Acting and made her professional stage debut in London in 1928 at the age of 19. Her early career was primarily focused on the British stage, where she honed her skills and established herself as a talented and versatile actress.

In the 1930s, Tandy married the actor Jack Hawkins, and they had a daughter. However, the marriage ended in divorce. In 1942, she married the Canadian actor Hume Cronyn, a partnership that would last for over five decades and have a profound impact on both their personal and professional lives.

Tandy and Cronyn moved to the United States in the 1940s, where they continued to work extensively on the stage, both individually and together. They became a renowned theatrical couple, performing in numerous Broadway productions and earning critical acclaim for their performances. Tandy received a Tony Award for her performance in *A Streetcar Named Desire* in 1948, further solidifying her reputation as a leading stage actress.

For decades, Tandy's career remained primarily focused on the stage. While she appeared in some film and television roles, she was primarily known for her work in the theatre. She and Cronyn collaborated on many projects, both on stage and in television, becoming a beloved and respected theatrical duo.

Despite her established career, mainstream film recognition eluded Tandy for many years. The film industry often favours younger actors, and Tandy, like many actresses of her generation, faced the challenges of an industry that often overlooked older women. However, she continued to pursue her craft with dedication and passion, never losing her love for acting.

The turning point in Tandy's film career came in the late 1980s with the play *Driving Miss Daisy*. Written by Alfred Uhry, the play tells the story of the evolving relationship between an elderly Jewish widow, Daisy Werthan, and her African American chauffeur, Hoke Colburn. Tandy originated the role of Daisy on stage, receiving widespread acclaim for her nuanced and heartfelt performance.

When *Driving Miss Daisy* was adapted into a film in 1989, Tandy reprised her role, alongside Morgan Freeman as Hoke Colburn. The film was a critical and commercial success, earning numerous awards, including the Academy Award for Best Picture.

Tandy's performance as Daisy Werthan was universally praised. She portrayed the character with grace, dignity, and a subtle vulnerability, capturing the complexities of an aging woman grappling with changing times and personal relationships. Her performance resonated deeply with audiences, earning her widespread recognition and admiration.

In 1990, Jessica Tandy achieved a remarkable milestone in her already distinguished acting career, winning the Academy Award for Best Actress for her poignant portrayal of Daisy Werthan in the film Driving Miss Daisy. At the age of 80, she became the oldest actress to ever win the award in that category, a feat that not only brought her international fame but also solidified her legacy as one of the most respected and admired actresses of her time. This achievement was not a sudden stroke of luck or a fleeting moment of recognition; it was the culmination of decades of dedicated work, unwavering commitment to her craft, and a persistent pursuit of excellence.

Tandy's acting career spanned over six decades, beginning in the British theatre in the 1920s. She and her husband, Hume Cronyn, were a renowned acting duo, achieving considerable success on the stage and later transitioning to film and television. However, it was her role in Driving Miss Daisy that brought her widespread mainstream recognition and cemented her place in cinematic history. The film, a heartwarming story about the unlikely friendship between an elderly Jewish widow and her African American chauffeur in the American South, resonated deeply with audiences and critics alike. Tandy's performance as the initially resistant and later deeply appreciative Daisy was lauded for its nuanced portrayal of aging, independence, and the evolving dynamics of human relationships.

This Academy Award win was significant for several reasons. It not only recognized Tandy's exceptional talent as an actress but also challenged prevailing societal notions about aging and the perceived limitations of older adults. It demonstrated that creative abilities and the capacity for outstanding performance do not diminish with age. On the contrary, Tandy's performance was enriched by her years of experience, her deep understanding of human emotions, and her ability to portray complex characters with depth and authenticity.

The award brought her international fame, introducing her work to a new generation of filmgoers who may not have been familiar with her earlier stage or screen roles. This newfound recognition further solidified her legacy as a respected and admired actress, ensuring that her contributions to the performing arts would be remembered and celebrated for years to come. It also provided a powerful message of hope and inspiration to aspiring actors and artists of all ages, demonstrating that recognition and success can come at any stage of life, even after decades of dedicated work.

Tandy's Oscar win was not just a personal triumph; it was a victory for older actors and actresses everywhere, challenging ageism in the entertainment industry and demonstrating the continued value and talent of experienced performers. It was a powerful reminder that the later years of life can be a time of significant achievement, recognition, and continued growth. Her story exemplifies the themes explored in this book, proving that one life, lived with dedication, passion, and perseverance, is indeed never too late to achieve one's dreams and leave a lasting mark on the world. It was a remarkable culmination of a long and dedicated career, a testament to the enduring power of talent and the potential for extraordinary achievements at any age.

Sadly, Tandy was diagnosed with ovarian cancer shortly before the release of *Driving Miss Daisy.* She continued to work despite her illness, but she passed away in 1994 at the age of 85.

Jessica Tandy's story provide us several key lessons:

- **Dedication to Craft** Tandy dedicated her life to the art of acting, honing her skills on the stage for decades before achieving mainstream film recognition. Her unwavering commitment to her craft was essential to her success.

- **Perseverance in the Face of Challenges** Tandy faced the challenges of an industry that often favours younger actors, but she never gave up on her passion. Her perseverance and resilience were crucial to her later-life success.

- **The Power of a Single Role** The role of Daisy Werthan proved to be a turning point in Tandy's career, bringing her widespread acclaim and recognition in the film industry. This demonstrates the power of a single role to redefine a career trajectory.

- **Talent Endures** Tandy's talent shone brightly throughout her career, but it was her later-life performance that brought her the greatest recognition. This proves that talent endures and that opportunities can arise at any stage of life.

- **The Importance of Partnership** Tandy's long and successful partnership with her husband, Hume Cronyn, played a significant role in her career. Their collaboration and mutual support contributed to both their individual and collective success.

Jessica Tandy's life and career serve as a powerful and inspiring reminder that recognition and acclaim can arrive at any stage of life, often unexpectedly in later years. While she had established a long and respected career in theatre, film, and television, it was her performance in Driving Miss Daisy, at the age of 80, that catapulted her to international fame and firmly cemented her place in cinematic history. This late-life triumph underscores the central theme of this book: that one life, lived with dedication, passion, and perseverance, is indeed never too late to shine and leave a lasting impact on the world.

Tandy's journey was not one of overnight success. She dedicated decades to honing her craft, beginning her acting career in the British theatre in the 1920s. She and her husband, Hume Cronyn, formed a renowned acting partnership, achieving considerable success on the stage and later transitioning to film and television. Throughout her career, she consistently delivered compelling performances, earning the respect of her peers and critics alike. However, it was her portrayal of Daisy Werthan, an aging Southern Jewish widow, that brought her widespread mainstream recognition and solidified her legacy.

Driving Miss Daisy resonated with audiences on a profound level, exploring themes of friendship, aging, prejudice, and social change in a poignant and heartwarming manner. Tandy's performance was particularly lauded for its nuanced portrayal of Daisy's character, capturing her initial resistance to change, her gradual acceptance of her chauffeur, and the deep bond that eventually develops between them. Her performance was not simply a portrayal of an elderly woman; it was a deeply human and relatable portrayal of the challenges and triumphs of aging, independence, and human connection.

Her Academy Award win at the age of 80 was more than just an award; it was a powerful statement that talent and artistry do not diminish with age. It challenged ageist stereotypes prevalent in the entertainment industry and demonstrated that profound and impactful performances can emerge at any point in an artist's career. This achievement was not a sudden stroke of luck but the culmination of a lifetime dedicated to the art of acting, a testament to her unwavering commitment to her craft. It proved that a truly timeless performance, one that resonates with audiences across generations, can arrive at any age, enriching the cultural landscape and inspiring others to pursue their own passions, regardless of their age.

Tandy's story embodies the spirit of this book, demonstrating that it's never too late to find one's purpose, to achieve recognition, or to make a lasting impact. Her Oscar win was not just a personal triumph; it was a celebration of a lifetime dedicated to the pursuit of artistic excellence. It serves as a powerful reminder that the potential for growth, achievement, and meaningful contribution continues throughout our lives, and that one life, lived with passion and dedication, is indeed never too late to shine brightly on the world stage.

11

Peter Mark Roget : The Architect of Words

"The mind, once stretched by a new idea, never returns to its original dimensions."

- Peter Mark Roget

Peter Mark Roget's name is inextricably linked with the *Thesaurus,* a cornerstone of writing and language for centuries. While he was a distinguished physician, scientist, and inventor, it was his later-life dedication to compiling this comprehensive collection of synonyms and antonyms that secured his enduring legacy. Roget's story is a testament to the power of long-held passions, the value of meticulous work, and the profound impact a single project can have on the world, even when undertaken later in life.

Born in London in 1779, Peter Mark Roget was a precocious child with a wide range of intellectual interests. He displayed a remarkable aptitude for learning and a keen curiosity about the world around him. His early life was marked by both intellectual stimulation and personal hardship. His father died when Roget was just four years old, a loss that deeply affected him and his family.

Despite these challenges, Roget pursued his education with diligence and determination. He studied medicine at the University of Edinburgh, graduating in 1798. He then returned to London and began his career as a physician. Roget's medical career was distinguished and varied. He served as a physician at the Manchester Infirmary and later at the Middlesex Hospital in London. He was also a lecturer in physiology at the Royal Institution.

Beyond his medical practice, Roget was deeply involved in scientific pursuits. He was elected a Fellow of the Royal Society in 1815 and served as its secretary from 1827 to 1849. He made significant contributions to various scientific fields, including optics, mathematics, and physiology. He even invented a slide rule specifically designed for calculations involving logarithmic scales.

However, amidst his diverse professional activities, Roget harboured a long-held personal interest: the organization and classification of words. This fascination stemmed from his youth, where he had begun compiling lists of words and their related concepts. He recognized the need for a systematic way to organize language, a tool that would aid writers and thinkers in finding the precise words to express their thoughts.

This idea, which would eventually become *Roget's Thesaurus*, occupied Roget's mind for decades. It wasn't a project he pursued actively during his busy years as a physician and scientist. It remained a personal pursuit, a passion that he returned to in his spare time.

The turning point came in Roget's retirement years. With more time at his disposal, he dedicated himself fully to the monumental task of compiling his thesaurus. This wasn't a quick or easy undertaking. It required years of meticulous research, painstaking organization, and careful categorization.

Roget's approach was innovative. He didn't simply create an alphabetical list of synonyms. Instead, he organized words and concepts into categories based on their semantic relationships. He created a system of conceptual categories, ranging from abstract notions like "existence" and "relation" to concrete concepts like "matter" and "intellect." Within each category, he listed synonyms and related words, providing a comprehensive and systematic way to explore the nuances of language.

The sheer scale of the project was immense. Roget meticulously researched and categorized thousands of words, ensuring accuracy and consistency throughout his work. He dedicated countless hours to refining his system, ensuring that it was both comprehensive and user-friendly.

In 1852, at the age of 73, Peter Mark Roget finally published the first edition of *Roget's Thesaurus of English Words and Phrases, Classified and Arranged so as to Facilitate the Expression of Ideas and Assist in Literary Composition.* [1] The book was an immediate success, [2] becoming a valuable resource for writers, speakers, and anyone seeking to express themselves with greater precision and clarity.

The *Thesaurus* has remained a standard reference work for over 150 years, undergoing numerous revisions and editions. It has become an indispensable tool for writers, students, and language enthusiasts worldwide, solidifying Roget's place in history as the architect of words.

Peter Mark Roget's story offers several important lessons:

- **The Power of Long-Held Passions** Roget's interest in organizing words began in his youth and remained a passion throughout his life. His dedication to this long-held interest led to his most significant achievement.

- **The Value of Meticulous Work** Compiling the *Thesaurus* was a monumental task that required years of meticulous research and organization.

Roget's dedication to detail was crucial to the success and enduring value of his work.

- **The Impact of Later-Life Pursuits** While Roget had a distinguished career in medicine and science, it was his later-life dedication to the *Thesaurus* that secured his lasting legacy. This demonstrates the profound impact that can be achieved through pursuing passions later in life.

- **Creating a Lasting Legacy** Roget's *Thesaurus* has had a profound impact on language and communication, becoming a standard reference work for generations. His story shows how a single project can have a lasting impact on the world.

- **Combining Diverse Interests** Roget's diverse interests in medicine, science, and language converged in his creation of the *Thesaurus.* This highlights the value of exploring different fields and finding connections between them.

Peter Mark Roget's story is a powerful reminder that it's never too late to pursue a passion project and make a significant contribution to the world. He dedicated his later years to a task that had fascinated him for decades, creating a resource that continues to be invaluable to this day. His journey perfectly exemplifies the theme of this book, proving that one life is indeed never too late to leave a lasting mark. He didn't just organize words; he organized thought, and in doing so, created a timeless tool that continues to empower expression.

12

Betty White: America's Golden Girl, A Timeless Spark

"You don't have to be born gifted to be successful. Success is about dedication, hard work, and sticking to it."

- Betty White

Betty White's career wasn't a flash in the pan; it was a slow burn that ignited into a brilliant and enduring flame. While she was a consistent presence on television for decades, her popularity and cultural icon status reached stratospheric heights in her later years, particularly with her iconic role as Rose Nylund on *The Golden Girls*. Her story is a testament to the power of longevity, adaptability, and the enduring appeal of genuine warmth and comedic talent. It's a powerful reminder that the spotlight can shine brightest later in life, illuminating a lifetime of dedication and hard work.

Born Betty Marion White in Oak Park, Illinois, in 1922, her family moved to Los Angeles during the Great Depression. From a young age, White displayed a natural inclination toward performing. She was drawn to writing and acting, participating in school plays and developing a love for the stage. This early passion would shape the course of her life and lead to a remarkable career in entertainment.

White's professional career began in the late 1930s with small roles in radio. During World War II, she served with the American Women's Voluntary Services. After the war, she transitioned to the burgeoning medium of television, a move that would prove pivotal in her career.

In the late 1940s, White began working in live television, a time when the medium was still in its infancy. She co-hosted a local Los Angeles television show called *Hollywood on Television* with Al Jarvis, gaining valuable experience in the fast-paced world of live broadcasting. This early experience honed her improvisational skills and laid the foundation for her future success in comedy.

In the 1950s, White starred in her first sitcom, *Life with Elizabeth,* which she also co-produced. This was a significant achievement for a woman in the early days of television, showcasing her talent not only as a performer but also as a producer. The show was a success, earning White her first Emmy Award nomination.

Throughout the 1960s and 1970s, White became a familiar face on television, appearing as a frequent guest on game shows like *Password, Match Game,* and *The $10,000 Pyramid.* Her quick wit, infectious laughter, and warm personality made her a popular guest, endearing her to audiences across the country. She also had recurring roles on various sitcoms, demonstrating her versatility as a comedic actress.

While White had a steady and successful career for decades, the turning point that catapulted her to a new level of fame came in 1985 with the premiere of *The Golden Girls.* At the age of 63, she took on the role of Rose Nylund, a sweet, naive, and often clueless widow from St. Olaf, Minnesota.

The Golden Girls, which also starred Bea Arthur, Rue McClanahan, and Estelle Getty, became a cultural phenomenon, resonating with audiences of all ages. The show's focus on the lives of four older women living together challenged conventional portrayals of aging on television, depicting them as vibrant, funny, and still very much engaged in life.

White's portrayal of Rose was a comedic masterpiece. Her impeccable timing, her ability to deliver deadpan lines with a twinkle in her eye, and her genuine warmth made Rose an instantly beloved character. The show's success brought White a new generation of fans and solidified her status as a comedic icon.

After *The Golden Girls* ended in 1992, White continued to work steadily in television, with guest appearances on numerous shows and recurring roles in sitcoms like *Suddenly Susan* and *Boston Legal.* She also became a popular commercial spokesperson, further cementing her status as a beloved public figure.

In the later years of her life, White experienced a remarkable resurgence in popularity, thanks in part to social media and a successful Snickers commercial that aired during the Super Bowl in 2010. This renewed attention brought her to the attention of younger audiences who were discovering her comedic genius for the first time.

White continued to work well into her 90s, appearing in films, television shows, and commercials. Her enduring popularity and her unwavering dedication to her craft made her a beloved figure in entertainment until her death in 2021 at the age of 99.

Betty White's story offers several important lessons:

- **Longevity and Adaptability** White's career spanned over seven decades, demonstrating the importance of longevity and adaptability in the entertainment industry. She successfully navigated the changing landscape of television, remaining relevant and popular throughout her career.

- **The Power of the Right Role** The role of Rose Nylund in *The Golden Girls* was a turning point in White's career, bringing her widespread acclaim and solidifying her status as a comedic icon. This demonstrates the power of finding the right role at the right time.
- **Staying True to Yourself** White's warm personality, genuine humour, and positive outlook resonated with audiences throughout her career. She remained true to herself, which contributed significantly to her enduring popularity.
- **Finding Success at Any Age** White's popularity reached new heights in her later years, proving that success and recognition can come at any stage of life. Her story is an inspiration to anyone who feels they've missed their "window of opportunity."
- **The Importance of Hard Work and Dedication** White's long and successful career was built on years of hard work, dedication, and a deep passion for her craft. This demonstrates the importance of perseverance in achieving long-term success.

Betty White's remarkable career stands as a vibrant testament to the enduring power of talent, warmth, and comedic timing, and most importantly, that it's never too late to shine brightly. While she enjoyed a long and successful career in television, beginning in the early days of the medium, it was her later-life success, particularly her iconic role as Rose Nylund in The Golden Girls, that cemented her status as a beloved cultural icon. This late-career resurgence not only brought her renewed fame but also solidified her place in television history, demonstrating that impact and recognition can arrive at any stage of life.

White's career began in radio and transitioned to television in its nascent stages. She was a pioneer in the medium, hosting her own live variety show in the 1950s and appearing on numerous game shows and sitcoms throughout the decades. She consistently showcased her comedic talents and warm personality, building a solid foundation of experience and establishing herself as a respected figure in the entertainment industry. However, it was her role in The Golden Girls, which premiered in 1985 when she was already in her 60s, that catapulted her to a new level of fame and adoration.

The Golden Girls resonated with audiences of all ages, offering a refreshing and humorous portrayal of aging, friendship, and female empowerment. White's portrayal of Rose, the sweet, naive, and often unintentionally hilarious Midwesterner, became an instant fan favourite. Her comedic timing, her ability to deliver deadpan humour with a touch of innocence, and her genuine warmth made Rose an unforgettable character. The show's success not only revitalized White's career but also challenged societal stereotypes about aging, portraying older women as vibrant, funny, and full of life.

This later-life success was not a mere stroke of good fortune; it was the result of decades of honing her craft, cultivating her comedic talents, and maintaining a positive and engaging presence. It was also a testament to her adaptability, her ability to connect with audiences across generations, and her willingness to embrace new opportunities. The Golden Girls became a cultural phenomenon, and White's role in its success solidified her status as "America's Golden Girl," a title that reflected her enduring popularity and her beloved persona.

White's journey embodies the very spirit of this book, demonstrating that one life is indeed never too late to achieve lasting impact. Her career wasn't just long; it was a dynamic and evolving journey marked by continuous growth, adaptation, and a consistent ability to connect with audiences. Her work is a testament to the enduring power of talent, warmth, and a timeless comedic spark—qualities that transcend age and continue to resonate with viewers. Her late-life success serves as an inspiration to anyone who feels they have missed their chance or that their dreams are no longer attainable, proving that it's never too late to shine brightly and leave a lasting mark on the world. Her story is a powerful reminder that the potential for creativity, joy, and meaningful contribution continues throughout our lives, and that one life, lived with passion and a genuine connection to others, is indeed never too late to achieve iconic status.

13
Julia Child : Mastering the Art of Late Blooming

"Find something you're passionate about and keep tremendously interested in it."

- Julia Child

Julia Child, a name synonymous with French cuisine in America, didn't discover her culinary destiny until later in life. Her journey, a delightful blend of passion, persistence, and a dash of serendipity, serves as a delicious example of late blooming. While she had various experiences before finding her true calling, it was in her late 30s, 40s, and 50s that she truly blossomed, revolutionizing American cooking and becoming a beloved cultural icon. Her story proves that it's never too late to find your passion and that even seemingly ordinary lives can take extraordinary turns.

Born Julia McWilliams in Pasadena, California, in 1912, her early life offered few hints of her future culinary fame. Tall and athletic, she enjoyed sports like basketball during her youth. She attended Smith College, graduating with a degree in history. Before and during World War II, she worked in advertising and media, a far cry from the kitchens of France. It wasn't until her marriage to Paul Child, a diplomat, and their subsequent move to Paris in 1948 that her life took a decisive culinary turn.

Paris, with its rich culinary heritage, became the catalyst for Child's transformation. Immersed in the vibrant food culture, she developed a deep fascination with French cuisine. This wasn't a casual interest; it was a full-blown immersion. She enrolled in the prestigious Le Cordon Bleu cooking school, embracing the rigorous training and immersing herself in the art of French cooking. This marked the beginning of her culinary education, a journey that would lead her to become one of the most influential figures in American culinary history.

It was in Paris that she met Simone Beck and Louisette Bertholle, two French women with a shared passion for sharing French cooking with Americans. Together, they embarked on an ambitious project: writing a comprehensive French cookbook tailored for American home cooks. This wasn't simply a translation of French recipes; it was an adaptation, taking into account the differences in ingredients, kitchen equipment, and culinary knowledge between the two cultures.

The creation of Mastering the Art of French Cooking was not a swift or effortless endeavour; it was a painstaking and protracted process, a labour of love that spanned several years of dedicated work by Julia Child, Simone Beck, and Louisette Bertholle. Their commitment to creating a definitive guide to French cuisine for American home cooks drove them to meticulously test and retest each recipe, ensuring not only its accuracy and authenticity but also its accessibility for cooks with varying levels of experience. They were determined to demystify French cooking, making it approachable and enjoyable for a wider audience.

This dedication to meticulous testing and retesting was a hallmark of their collaborative process. They understood that translating complex French culinary techniques into clear and concise instructions for American home cooks required rigorous experimentation. They wanted to ensure that each recipe worked flawlessly, producing consistently delicious results, regardless of the cook's skill level. This involved not only testing the recipes themselves but also adapting them to readily available American ingredients and kitchen equipment. This painstaking process required countless hours in the kitchen, experimenting with different techniques, adjusting ingredient quantities, and meticulously documenting each step.

Their dedication to detail extended beyond the recipes themselves. They were determined to create a comprehensive guide that covered all aspects of French cooking, from basic techniques to complex dishes. This resulted in a massive and highly detailed manuscript, a testament to their thoroughness and dedication. However, this very comprehensiveness presented a significant challenge: finding a publisher willing to take on such a large and complex project.

The manuscript, with its extensive length and detailed instructions, proved to be a difficult sell in the publishing world. Many publishers deemed it too long, too complex, and too focused on what they perceived as a niche market. They doubted that there was a sufficient audience for such a comprehensive and technical cookbook. This rejection was undoubtedly discouraging, but the trio refused to be deterred. They firmly believed in the value of their work, recognizing the potential it had to transform the way Americans cooked and appreciated French cuisine.

This unwavering belief in their project fuelled their persistence. They continued to refine their manuscript, seeking out new publishers and tirelessly advocating for their work. They were convinced that there was an audience eager to learn the art of French cooking, and they were determined to bring their knowledge and passion to that audience. This persistence, this refusal to give up in the face of rejection, ultimately proved to be the key to their success. It demonstrates the importance of unwavering belief in one's vision, especially when facing obstacles and setbacks. Their dedication to accuracy, accessibility, and comprehensiveness, coupled with their unwavering belief in the value of their work, ultimately led to the publication of Mastering the Art of French Cooking, a cookbook that would revolutionize American home cooking and solidify their place in culinary history.

Finally, in 1961, Alfred A. Knopf published *Mastering the Art of French Cooking*. The book was an immediate sensation, becoming a culinary bible for American cooks eager to explore the world of French cuisine. It demystified complex techniques, provided clear and concise instructions, and instilled confidence in home cooks to tackle dishes they might have previously considered too daunting.

The success of the cookbook led to another pivotal moment in Child's career: her transition to television. In 1963, she debuted her own cooking show, *The French Chef*, on public television. This was a groundbreaking move, bringing French cooking directly into American homes. Child's personality shone through on screen. She was enthusiastic, unpretentious, and endearingly clumsy, making her relatable and approachable to viewers. She wasn't afraid to make mistakes, famously saying, "If you're alone in the kitchen and you drop the lamb, who's going to see?," turning kitchen mishaps into charming moments.

Child's transition to television wasn't without its challenges. She had to adapt her style to the visual medium, learning to communicate effectively to a camera. However, her natural charisma and her genuine passion for cooking quickly won over audiences. *The French Chef* became a hit, popularizing cooking shows and making Child a household name.

Julia Child's achievements are numerous and significant. *Mastering the Art of French Cooking* remains a classic, influencing generations of cooks. *The French Chef* paved the way for the modern cooking show, transforming the way Americans approach food and cooking. Child herself became a cultural icon, celebrated for her enthusiastic personality, her practical approach to cooking, and her ability to demystify French cuisine. She continued to write cookbooks and host television shows for decades, leaving a lasting legacy on American culinary culture.

Child's story offers several valuable lessons applicable to anyone pursuing a passion, especially later in life. First, it demonstrates that passions can be discovered at any age. Her love for cooking didn't truly ignite until her late 30s, proving that it's never too late to find your calling. Second, it highlights the importance of persistence and collaboration. The years of work on the cookbook and the collaboration with her co-authors were essential to its success. Third, it showcases the value of embracing new challenges. Child's transition to television was a bold move that paid off immensely, demonstrating the rewards of stepping outside one's comfort zone. Fourth, it underscores the importance of making expertise accessible. Child's ability to demystify complex culinary techniques made French cooking approachable for a wider audience. Finally, and perhaps most importantly, it demonstrates the power of authenticity and enthusiasm. Child's genuine passion for cooking and her warm, approachable personality were key to her success, both in print and on screen.

Julia Child's life story is a vibrant and inspiring testament to the power of late blooming, demonstrating that discovering one's true calling and achieving extraordinary success can happen at any age. She didn't find her passion for cooking until her late 30s, a period when many individuals have already established their careers. Yet, through unwavering dedication, infectious enthusiasm, and a relentless pursuit of culinary excellence, she transformed the American culinary landscape, making French cuisine accessible and enjoyable for home cooks across the nation. Her journey is a delicious reminder that one life is indeed never too late to find your passion and achieve remarkable things.

Prior to discovering her love for cooking, Child led a varied life, working in advertising, media, and even for the Office of Strategic Services during World War II. It wasn't until she moved to Paris with her husband in her late 30s that she experienced a culinary awakening. Immersed in French culture and cuisine, she enrolled in Le Cordon Bleu cooking school, embarking on a transformative journey that would change the course of her life. This late-life discovery of her passion was not a carefully planned career move; it was a serendipitous encounter that ignited a lifelong love affair with food and cooking.

Child's dedication to mastering French cooking was unwavering. She immersed herself in the culinary world, studying diligently, experimenting with recipes, and collaborating with Simone Beck and Louisette Bertholle to write Mastering the Art of French Cooking. This monumental work, published in 1961, was a game-changer for American home cooks. It demystified French cuisine, translating complex techniques and recipes into clear and accessible instructions, empowering ordinary individuals to create delicious French dishes in their own kitchens.

Her subsequent television show, The French Chef, further cemented her status as a culinary icon. Her warm and engaging personality, her unpretentious approach to cooking, and her willingness to embrace mistakes made her an instant hit with viewers. She didn't just teach America to cook French food; she taught America to embrace the joy of cooking, to find pleasure in the process, and to not be afraid to experiment and have fun in the kitchen. She normalized making mistakes, demonstrating that even culinary mishaps could be learning experiences.

Child's impact on American culture extends far beyond simply popularizing French cuisine. She inspired a generation of home cooks to embrace their own culinary creativity, to find joy in the act of cooking, and to appreciate the pleasures of sharing good food with friends and family. She proved that even a late start can lead to a truly masterful career, not just in the culinary arts but in any field. Her story is a powerful reminder that passion, dedication, and a willingness to embrace new challenges can lead to extraordinary achievements at any age. Her life is a delicious reminder that one life is indeed never too late to discover one's true calling and leave a lasting and flavourful mark on the world.

14

Henry Ford: Beyond the Model T, A Legacy of Innovation

"Obstacles are those frightful things you see when you take your eyes off your goal."

- Henry Ford

Henry Ford's name is synonymous with the automobile, revolutionizing transportation and shaping the 20th century. While his early achievements, particularly the mass production of the Model T, are widely celebrated, his later life revealed a continued drive for innovation, a broader vision that extended beyond the car, and a complex legacy that continues to be debated. This chapter explores Henry Ford's "second act," demonstrating that his innovative spirit didn't cease with the Model T, but rather evolved into new areas of focus, leaving a lasting impact on various facets of American life.

Born on a farm in Greenfield Township, Michigan, in 1863, Henry Ford displayed a distinct disinterest in farm work and a fascination with machinery from a young age. He was captivated by the workings of engines and mechanical devices, a passion that would ultimately define his life's work. In 1879, he left the farm to apprentice as a machinist in Detroit, a pivotal step in his journey toward becoming a pioneer in the automotive industry.

Ford's early career involved working as an engineer for the Edison Illuminating Company, gaining valuable experience with electricity and engineering principles. However, his true passion lay in developing a practical and affordable automobile. He experimented with various engine designs and prototypes, driven by a vision of making cars accessible to the masses.

In 1903, Ford founded the Ford Motor Company, a venture that would forever change the landscape of transportation. His focus was on efficiency and affordability, leading to the development of the assembly line and the mass production of the Model T. This innovation dramatically reduced the cost of automobiles, making them accessible to a wider segment of the population and ushering in the era of mass car ownership.

The Model T became an icon of American industry, transforming not only transportation but also the social and economic fabric of the nation. It created new industries, spurred the growth of suburbs, and fundamentally altered the way people lived and worked. Ford's success with the Model T made him a household name and a symbol of American ingenuity.

However, after achieving this monumental success, Ford didn't simply rest on his laurels. His later life, often overshadowed by the Model T era, saw him pursue new ventures and expand his vision beyond the automobile. This "second act" revealed a continued drive to innovate and a broader interest in social and economic issues.

One of Henry Ford's most notable later-life endeavours, demonstrating his continued drive for innovation and his belief in the power of technology to transform society, was his foray into the field of aviation. Just as he had revolutionized personal transportation with the automobile, Ford envisioned a similar revolution in air travel. He believed that airplanes held immense potential to connect people and facilitate commerce on a global scale, and he dedicated significant resources to the development and advancement of aircraft technology.

Ford's commitment to aviation was not a fleeting interest; he invested heavily in research, development, and manufacturing, establishing the Ford Airplane Division in 1925. This venture was not simply a side project; it was a serious commitment to pushing the boundaries of aviation technology and contributing to the growth of the nascent aviation industry. His most significant contribution to this field was the development of the Ford Trimotor, an all-metal, three-engine airplane that played a pivotal role in the early days of commercial aviation.

The Ford Trimotor, affectionately nicknamed the "Tin Goose" due to its corrugated aluminum skin, was a groundbreaking aircraft for its time. Unlike earlier airplanes that were primarily constructed from wood and fabric, the Trimotor's all-metal construction made it significantly stronger, more durable, and less susceptible to the elements. This innovation was a major advancement in aircraft design, paving the way for the modern all-metal airplanes we see today.

The Trimotor's reliability and durability quickly earned it a reputation as a workhorse for airlines. It could carry a significant number of passengers and cargo, and its three engines provided a greater margin of safety compared to single-engine aircraft. This reliability was crucial in establishing public trust in air travel, which was still a relatively new and somewhat risky mode of transportation at the time. The Trimotor became a popular choice for airlines across the United States and around the world, playing a key role in the development of commercial air routes and the expansion of air travel as a viable and practical means of transportation.

Ford's involvement in aviation was not just about building airplanes; it was about creating a complete system for air travel. He invested in the development of airports and airfields, recognizing the importance of infrastructure in supporting the growth of the industry. He also contributed to the development of airmail services, further demonstrating his belief in the potential of aviation to connect people and facilitate commerce.

While Ford's primary legacy remains his contributions to the automobile industry, his foray into aviation demonstrates his continued drive for innovation and his vision for the future of transportation. The Ford Trimotor played a crucial role in the early development of commercial aviation, helping to establish air travel as a safe, reliable, and practical mode of transportation. This later-life endeavour further exemplifies Ford's commitment to progress and his belief in the transformative power of technology, illustrating that his innovative spirit extended beyond the realm of automobiles and into the vast expanse of the skies.

Ford also turned his attention to agriculture, believing that industrial principles could be applied to farming to increase efficiency and productivity. He promoted the use of tractors and other mechanized farm equipment, contributing to the modernization of agriculture. He also explored the use of soybeans for various industrial products, demonstrating his interest in finding innovative uses for agricultural resources.

Another significant aspect of Ford's later life was his focus on what he called "village industries." This concept aimed to decentralize manufacturing and provide employment opportunities in rural areas. He established small factories in rural communities, providing jobs for farmers and their families during the off-season and helping to revitalize rural economies.

Furthermore, Ford established the Henry Ford Hospital in Detroit, a leading medical institution that continues to provide high-quality healthcare. He also founded the Henry Ford Museum and Greenfield Village, a vast complex dedicated to preserving American history and showcasing the evolution of technology and industry. These philanthropic endeavors demonstrate Ford's commitment to education, healthcare, and the preservation of American heritage.

Despite these later-life pursuits, Ford's later years were also marked by controversies. His management style became increasingly autocratic, and his views on social and political issues were often controversial. These aspects of his later life have contributed to a complex and nuanced understanding of his legacy.

Henry Ford's "second act" offers several important lessons of life.

- **Continued Innovation** Ford's drive to innovate didn't end with the Model T. He continued to explore new technologies and industries, demonstrating the importance of continuous learning and adaptation.
- **Expanding Vision** Ford's vision extended beyond the automobile to encompass aviation, agriculture, and social reform. This demonstrates the power of expanding one's perspective and seeking new avenues for contribution.
- **The Importance of Philanthropy** Ford's establishment of the Henry Ford Hospital and the Henry Ford Museum and Greenfield Village

demonstrates the lasting impact that philanthropy can have on society.

- **A Complex Legacy** Ford's later life was marked by both significant achievements and controversies, highlighting the complexity of human character and the importance of considering the full context of an individual's life and work.
- **Beyond Initial Success** Ford's story shows that success is not a static point but a continuous process of evolution and adaptation. It demonstrates the importance of continuing to learn, grow, and contribute throughout one's life.

Henry Ford's story is a powerful reminder that achievement and contribution are not limited to a single period in life. While his early success with the Model T cemented his place in history, his later-life pursuits revealed a continued drive for innovation and a broader vision for impacting society. His journey embodies the spirit of this book, demonstrating that one life is indeed never too late to explore new avenues, contribute to the world, and build a lasting legacy. He showed the world that even after changing it once, one can still find new ways to innovate and leave a mark.

15

Dharam Pal Singh Gulati : The Spice King of India

"Never give up on a dream just because of the time it will take to accomplish it. The time will pass anyway."

- Dharampal Singh Gulati

Dharam Pal Singh Gulati's life story is a potent blend of resilience, entrepreneurial spirit, and the unwavering pursuit of a dream, proving that success can indeed be a late-life bloom. His journey, from a small spice shop in pre-partition India to a multi-million dollar empire, is not just a business success story; it's an inspiring narrative of overcoming adversity and building a lasting legacy. Unlike many entrepreneurs who find success in their youth, Gulati's most significant achievements unfolded in his later years, demonstrating that experience, hard work, and a keen understanding of the market can lead to remarkable outcomes, regardless of age.

From Sialkot to Delhi: A Foundation of Resilience

Dharam Pal Gulati's life began in Sialkot, a city now located in Pakistan, in 1923. His early years were closely connected to his family's established spice business, "Mahashian Di Hatti" (MDH), meaning "Shop of Respectable Men." This early immersion in the world of spices, from the sourcing and blending to the selling and customer interactions, provided him with a foundational understanding of the trade that would later prove invaluable. He absorbed not only the technical aspects of the business but also the importance of quality, customer service, and the value of a strong brand reputation. This early exposure was more than just a family business; it was an education that laid the groundwork for his future entrepreneurial endeavors.

The year 1947 brought a dramatic and life-altering event: the partition of India. This tumultuous period of political division and widespread violence resulted in the displacement of millions of people, including Gulati and his family. Forced to leave their established life and business behind in Sialkot, they became refugees in Delhi, India. This displacement was not merely a change of location; it was a complete disruption of their lives, forcing them to confront the daunting task of rebuilding everything from scratch. They faced immense financial instability, navigating a new and unfamiliar environment with limited resources. This period of hardship tested their resilience and forced them to adapt to drastically changed circumstances.

In the face of these immense challenges, Gulati demonstrated remarkable resourcefulness and unwavering determination. He didn't succumb to despair or resignation; instead, he took on a variety of odd jobs to support his family, including driving a tonga (a horse-drawn carriage). This willingness to take on any work available, regardless of its perceived status, speaks volumes about his character and his commitment to providing for his loved ones. These experiences, though difficult, proved to be instrumental in shaping his future success. They instilled in him a deep understanding of the value of hard work, the importance of adaptability, and the ability to overcome adversity. The challenges of rebuilding his life after partition forged a resilient spirit that would become a defining characteristic of his entrepreneurial journey. This period wasn't just about survival; it was a crucial training ground that honed the qualities that would later drive his success in the spice business. It taught him the importance of perseverance, the power of adaptability, and the unwavering determination to overcome any obstacle in his path. This foundation of resilience, born from hardship and displacement, would ultimately become a cornerstone of his later triumphs.

Re-establishing the Family Legacy: A Focus on Quality

In 1948, Dharam Pal Gulati took a decisive and pivotal step, re-establishing the family spice business in Delhi under the familiar and cherished MDH (Mahashian Di Hatti) brand name. This act was far more significant than simply recreating a lost livelihood after the upheaval of partition; it was a strategic move to capitalize on a pre-existing market awareness and to revive a valued family legacy. By retaining the MDH name, Gulati tapped into the memories and associations that customers had with the original business in Sialkot, providing a sense of continuity and trust in a time of great change and uncertainty. This was a crucial foundation upon which to rebuild.

From the very beginning of this new venture, Gulati prioritized quality above all other considerations. He understood that in a market saturated with various spice vendors, offering consistently superior quality would be the key differentiator. This wasn't a mere marketing slogan; it was a deeply ingrained principle that guided every aspect of his operations. He personally oversaw the grinding and blending of spices, meticulously ensuring that every product met his exacting standards. This hands-on approach, while demanding, allowed him to maintain complete control over the quality of the final product, from the sourcing of raw materials to the final packaging. By personally being involved in the production process, he ensured that the quality of MDH spices remained consistent, batch after batch.

This unwavering commitment to quality became a cornerstone of the MDH brand, setting it apart from competitors in the marketplace. While other vendors might have focused on lower prices or faster production, Gulati prioritized the aroma, flavour, and purity of his spices. This dedication to quality resonated strongly with consumers, who quickly recognized the difference. This difference in quality was not simply about taste; it was about trust. Customers knew that when they purchased MDH spices, they were getting a product that was consistently high in quality, free from adulterants, and true to its traditional flavour profile.

This focus on quality was not merely a shrewd business tactic; it was a genuine reflection of Gulati's personal values and his deep respect for the family tradition. He understood that the MDH name represented more than just a business; it represented a legacy of quality, integrity, and service that had been passed down through generations. By upholding these values, he not only built a successful business but also honoured his family's heritage. This blend of personal values and business acumen proved to be a powerful combination, driving the growth and success of the MDH brand for decades to come. He understood that building trust with customers was paramount, and consistent quality was the most effective way to achieve this. By delivering on his promise of superior spices, Gulati cultivated a loyal customer base that would remain with the brand for generations.

Expanding the Reach : Strategic Marketing and Personal Branding

Gulati's vision for MDH was not limited to the confines of his local Delhi community. He possessed a keen understanding of market dynamics and recognized the potential for significant growth beyond his initial customer base. This foresight led him to strategically focus on two key areas: product diversification and distribution network expansion. He understood that catering to a wider range of tastes and culinary needs would be crucial for expanding MDH's market share. Therefore, he progressively broadened the product range, moving beyond basic ground spices to offer a diverse array of pre-mixed spice blends and seasonings tailored to specific regional cuisines and dishes. This diversification not only appealed to a larger customer base but also simplified the cooking process for consumers, offering convenient and flavourful solutions for a variety of culinary creations. This strategic move allowed MDH to establish a stronger foothold within the competitive spice industry.

Equally crucial to Gulati's expansion strategy was his focus on building a robust and efficient distribution network. He recognized that even the highest quality products would be ineffective if they were not readily accessible to consumers. He meticulously developed a distribution system that ensured MDH products were available not only in Delhi but also across India and, eventually, internationally. This strategic expansion allowed the brand to reach new customers in diverse markets, solidifying its position as a leading spice provider on both a national and global scale. This foresight in developing a comprehensive distribution network was a key factor in MDH's transition from a local business to a major player in the spice industry.

Perhaps one of Gulati's most brilliant strategic moves, and a key element of MDH's enduring success, was his decision to become the face of the brand. This wasn't a calculated marketing ploy devised by an advertising agency; it was an authentic representation of Gulati himself. His distinctive appearance–the traditional turban, the impeccable white attire, and his warm, grandfatherly demeanour–became instantly recognizable and deeply associated with MDH. This personal branding created a powerful emotional connection with consumers. It wasn't just an image; it was a symbol of trust, authenticity, and a sense of family tradition, resonating deeply with Indian cultural values.

His consistent presence in MDH commercials and advertisements, often showcasing him actively participating in the spice-making process or interacting with customers, further strengthened this connection. This personal touch transformed MDH from a mere product into a beloved household name. Consumers didn't just buy MDH spices; they bought into the story of a dedicated entrepreneur, a family tradition, and a commitment to quality. This strategy was particularly effective in a market where trust and authenticity are highly valued. By presenting himself as the embodiment of the brand, Gulati instilled a sense of confidence and loyalty in consumers, creating a lasting bond that transcended mere commercial transactions. This personal connection, combined with the consistent high quality of the products, was instrumental in establishing MDH as a dominant force in the spice market.

A Lasting Legacy: From Spices to an Empire

Dharam Pal Gulati's life story stands as a powerful and inspiring testament to the remarkable potential for late-life entrepreneurial success. Unlike many business leaders who achieve prominence in their youth, Gulati's journey to widespread recognition and the building of his multi-million dollar spice empire unfolded primarily in his later years. This fact alone makes his story particularly compelling, demonstrating that dedication, unwavering hard work, and an unshakeable belief in one's product or vision can indeed lead to extraordinary achievements, even after facing significant setbacks, displacement, and the need to start over later in life. His experience defies the common misconception that entrepreneurial success is solely a young person's game, offering hope and inspiration to those who may feel they have missed their chance.

Gulati's path was not without its challenges. The partition of India in 1947 forced him and his family to rebuild their lives from scratch, a deeply disruptive and emotionally taxing experience. However, this adversity did not deter him; instead, it fuelled his determination to recreate the family spice business, MDH, in Delhi. This act of rebuilding was not simply about restoring a lost livelihood; it was a testament to his resilience and his unwavering belief in the value of his family's heritage and the quality of their product.

His strategic approach to building MDH was multifaceted and remarkably effective. He understood that quality would be the cornerstone of his brand, personally overseeing the production process to ensure consistency and excellence. This commitment to quality differentiated MDH from its competitors and fostered a loyal customer base. Beyond quality, Gulati recognized the importance of expansion, both in terms of product range and distribution. He broadened the offerings to cater to diverse tastes and strategically built a distribution network that reached customers across India and eventually the globe.

Perhaps his most ingenious strategic move was his decision to become the face of the MDH brand. His distinctive appearance and warm, grandfatherly demeanour created a powerful emotional connection with consumers. This personal branding wasn't a contrived marketing tactic; it was an authentic reflection of Gulati's personality and values. His presence in advertisements conveyed trust, authenticity, and a sense of family tradition, transforming MDH from a mere product into a beloved household name. This personal connection, combined with consistent quality and strategic expansion, proved to be a winning formula.

Gulati's journey is a powerful embodiment of the spirit of late blooming, demonstrating that one life is indeed never too late to achieve one's dreams and leave a lasting impact on the business world. He didn't just sell spices; he built a brand that became a cultural icon, a testament to the power of vision, perseverance, and strategic marketing. His story continues to inspire entrepreneurs and individuals of all ages, demonstrating that the pursuit of a dream, combined with hard work, a strategic approach, and an unwavering belief in oneself, can lead to extraordinary achievements, regardless of when that journey begins. His story is a powerful affirmation that the potential for success and lasting impact is not limited by age or circumstance.

16

The Uncommon Thread: What Sets Them Apart

"The greatest glory in living lies not in never falling, but in rising every time we fall."

- Nelson Mandela

The individuals profiled in this book, from Ray Kroc to Betty White, from Diana Nyad to Peter Mark Roget, represent a diverse tapestry of achievements, spanning various fields and spanning decades of life. Yet, despite their different backgrounds and pursuits, a common thread weaves through their stories, connecting them and distinguishing them from the ordinary. This chapter delves into those shared qualities, exploring what set these individuals apart and what lessons we can glean from their extraordinary lives.

Unwavering persistence stands as a cornerstone characteristic shared by the extraordinary individuals profiled in this book. It serves as the driving force propelling them through adversity, the unwavering fuel that sustains their dreams even amidst repeated setbacks and profound moments of doubt. This quality transcends mere repetition of effort; it embodies a deep-seated refusal to accept defeat, a relentless pursuit of a vision that overshadows temporary obstacles. Their narratives are not sanitized tales of effortless triumph; they are authentic, gritty accounts of struggle, resilience, and the unwavering commitment necessary to achieve remarkable feats. Persistence, in this context, is not a static trait but a dynamic process comprising several key elements. It begins with a clarity of vision, a well-defined and compelling picture of the desired outcome. This vision acts as a constant source of motivation, a guiding star that keeps them on course even when the path becomes obscured by challenges. Coupled with this clear vision is an unwavering belief in the possibility of its realization. Despite facing seemingly insurmountable odds, these individuals maintained a fundamental conviction that their goals were attainable. This unwavering belief fueled their determination and provided the courage to persevere.

Furthermore, persistence is intertwined with adaptability and a willingness to learn. It is not a blind repetition of the same actions, regardless of the outcome. Instead, it involves a continuous process of adjusting strategies, gleaning lessons from mistakes, and constantly refining the approach. These individuals demonstrated a remarkable capacity for adaptation, willing to modify their methods based on feedback and experience, showcasing a pragmatic and flexible approach to achieving their objectives. Perhaps most importantly, the journey toward ambitious goals demands significant emotional fortitude. It requires the ability to withstand the inevitable storms of setbacks, rejections, and moments of self-doubt. These individuals possessed a remarkable capacity to manage their emotions, maintaining a positive outlook and demonstrating the resilience needed to bounce back from adversity.

Ray Kroc's trajectory epitomizes the power of persistence in the business world. He was not the originator of McDonald's; he was a milkshake machine salesman who recognized the untapped potential of the McDonald brothers' efficient system. However, transforming this potential into a global fast-food empire required relentless effort. Kroc faced countless rejections from financial institutions, potential investors, and prospective franchisees. Yet, driven by his unwavering belief in the McDonald's system and his expansive vision of a nationwide chain, he persistently knocked on doors, meticulously refined his business pitch, and tenaciously overcame every obstacle that stood in his way. His unwavering persistence, even in the face of repeated setbacks, proved to be the linchpin of his ultimate triumph.

Diana Nyad's relentless pursuit of the Cuba-Florida swim provides a compelling example of physical and mental persistence. The arduous 103-mile journey across the treacherous Florida Straits presents a formidable challenge, even for the most seasoned swimmers. Nyad faced not a single setback, but multiple failed attempts, enduring extreme physical exhaustion, agonizing jellyfish stings, and unpredictable, often hostile, weather conditions. Each of these failures could have easily served as a justification to abandon her seemingly impossible dream. Yet, she consistently returned to the water, fueled by a deep-seated desire to conquer the challenge and prove that age is not a barrier to extraordinary achievement. Her eventual success at the age of 64 stands as a powerful testament to the transformative power of unwavering persistence in the face of seemingly insurmountable odds.

Colonel Sanders' story offers a poignant illustration of persistence in the context of financial hardship and a late-life career change. Facing financial ruin in his 60s after a new highway diverted traffic away from his established restaurant, he found himself at a crossroads. He could have easily succumbed to despair and accepted his seemingly bleak fate. Instead, he embarked on a tireless, cross-country journey to franchise his carefully crafted chicken recipe. Enduring numerous rejections from skeptical restaurant owners, often sleeping in his car to save money, he never relinquished his belief in the quality and marketability of his product. His tenacious persistence, even in the face of late-life adversity, ultimately paved the way for the creation of the Kentucky Fried Chicken empire, a global success story born from the ashes of financial hardship.

These narratives, along with the other stories presented within this book, are not romanticized accounts of instant success. They represent real-life journeys marked by struggle, perseverance, and the unwavering commitment required to achieve extraordinary outcomes. They demonstrate that persistence is not simply about trying again; it is about a deep-seated refusal to surrender one's dreams, a willingness to learn and adapt from every setback, and the development of the emotional fortitude necessary to keep moving forward, even when the odds seem insurmountable. It is this unwavering persistence, this tenacious refusal to give up, that often distinguishes those who achieve extraordinary things from those who only dream of them.

Closely linked to persistence is a strong sense of purpose. These individuals were not simply pursuing fleeting whims or superficial goals. They were driven by a deep inner conviction, a sense of purpose that fueled their actions and sustained them through difficult times. For Fauja Singh, running became a way to cope with grief and find new meaning in life. For Peter Mark Roget, the *Thesaurus* was more than just a book; it was a passion project, a way to organize knowledge and empower communication. Betty White's decades-long career wasn't just about seeking fame; it was about sharing her comedic talent and bringing joy to audiences. This clear sense of purpose provided a compass, guiding their actions and providing the motivation to overcome obstacles.

Adaptability stands as another crucial quality woven into the fabric of the lives of those who achieve significant success, particularly later in life. The world is in a constant state of flux, a dynamic environment characterized by evolving technologies, shifting societal norms, and unforeseen circumstances. In such a world, the ability to adapt, to adjust one's strategies, and to embrace new possibilities becomes not just an advantage but a necessity for sustained success. The individuals profiled in this book exemplify this quality, demonstrating a remarkable capacity to navigate change and thrive in a dynamic world. Adaptability, in this context, is not simply about reacting to change; it's about proactively anticipating it, embracing it, and leveraging it to one's advantage. It encompasses several key components:

A core element of adaptability is a willingness to learn and unlearn. The world is constantly presenting new information and new ways of doing things. Those who are adaptable are open to acquiring new knowledge, embracing new skills, and even discarding old habits or beliefs that no longer serve them. This requires a certain humility, a recognition that there is always more to learn, and a willingness to step outside one's comfort zone. It also requires the ability to critically evaluate existing knowledge and be willing to let go of outdated or ineffective practices.

Another important aspect of adaptability is flexibility in thinking and approach. Rigid adherence to a single plan or strategy can be detrimental in a changing world. Adaptable individuals are able to think creatively, consider multiple perspectives, and adjust their course of action as needed. They are comfortable with ambiguity and uncertainty, and they are able to pivot quickly when faced with unexpected challenges or opportunities. This flexibility allows them to navigate complex situations effectively and to capitalize on emerging trends.

Furthermore, adaptability involves embracing new technologies and tools. Technological advancements are constantly transforming industries and creating new possibilities. Adaptable individuals are not resistant to these changes; they embrace them, learning how to use new technologies to enhance their work, reach new audiences, and achieve their goals more effectively. This willingness to adopt new tools and techniques allows them to stay relevant and competitive in a rapidly evolving world.

Ray Kroc's success with McDonald's is a prime example of adaptability in the business world. While he was deeply committed to the core principles of the McDonald's system–speed, efficiency, and consistency–he was also willing to adapt the menu and marketing strategies to meet changing consumer preferences. He introduced new menu items, adjusted advertising campaigns, and embraced new technologies to keep McDonald's relevant and appealing to evolving tastes. This adaptability was crucial to the company's continued growth and global success.

Henry Ford, after revolutionizing automobile production with the Model T and the assembly line, demonstrated adaptability by turning his attention to other ventures. He recognized the potential of aviation and invested heavily in the development of aircraft, recognizing the future of transportation extended beyond ground vehicles. He also explored new applications for agricultural products, demonstrating a willingness to explore new frontiers and adapt his focus beyond his initial success in the automotive industry. This willingness to explore new areas of innovation demonstrated a key adaptability that kept him relevant in broader industrial and societal contexts.

Betty White's remarkable career in television provides a compelling example of adaptability in the entertainment industry. She navigated the evolving landscape of television for over seven decades, transitioning seamlessly from live broadcasts in the early days of television to sitcoms, game sshows, talk show appearances, and even embracing social media in her later years. She continually found new ways to connect with audiences across generations, adapting her comedic style and persona to remain relevant and beloved throughout her long career. This adaptability was essential to her enduring popularity and her status as a cultural icon.

These examples highlight the importance of adaptability as a key ingredient for success, especially in the context of late-life achievements. The ability to learn and unlearn, to think flexibly, and to embrace new technologies allows individuals to remain relevant, capitalize on new opportunities, and continue to thrive in a constantly changing world. Adaptability is not merely a reactive response to change; it's a proactive mindset that allows individuals to shape their own destinies and achieve extraordinary things, regardless of their age or circumstances. It is this capacity for adaptation that allows individuals to remain relevant, effective, and successful throughout their lives, transforming potential challenges into opportunities for growth and achievement.

A powerful internal force propelling the achievements of the individuals profiled in this book is an unwavering belief in themselves and their vision. This self-belief functions as an internal compass, guiding their actions and providing the resilience necessary to navigate the inevitable challenges encountered on the path to realizing ambitious goals. These individuals were not easily swayed by external criticism or internal self-doubt. They possessed a clear and compelling vision of their desired outcomes, coupled with a deep, unwavering conviction in their capacity to transform that vision into tangible reality. This self-assurance was not rooted in arrogance or naive optimism; rather, it stemmed from a profound understanding of their own strengths, a realistic appraisal of the challenges that lay ahead, and a resolute determination to overcome them. This internal fortitude is especially crucial when pursuing unconventional or ambitious goals that may attract skepticism, or even outright ridicule, from others.

This robust self-belief manifests itself in several key ways. First, it provides a clear internal compass, a strong sense of direction rooted in a deep understanding of one's values, passions, and objectives. This internal guidance system provides a sense of purpose and direction, informing decisions and shaping actions even amidst uncertainty or external pressure. Second, it builds resilience against external criticism. The pursuit of ambitious goals often invites scrutiny, skepticism, and even derision from those who may not understand or share the same vision. Individuals with strong self-belief possess the ability to filter out this negativity, recognizing that such criticism often stems from the limitations or fears of others rather than an objective assessment of their own abilities. This allows them to maintain focus and continue pursuing their vision undeterred by external doubts.

Third, robust self-belief provides the tools to overcome self-doubt. Internal self-doubt is a common human experience, particularly when confronting challenging tasks or venturing into unfamiliar territory.However, individuals with strong self-belief are equipped to manage these internal anxieties and prevent them from undermining their efforts. They are adept at recognizing negative self-talk, challenging its validity through reasoned self-assessment, and replacing it with positive affirmations and a focus on their inherent strengths. Finally, this self-belief allows individuals to embrace challenges as opportunities for growth. Difficulties are not perceived as insurmountable obstacles but rather as valuable opportunities for learning, development, and refinement. This mindset allows them to approach challenges with curiosity and determination rather than fear and avoidance, viewing setbacks as temporary detours rather than definitive dead ends.

Diana Nyad's relentless pursuit of the Cuba-Florida swim provides a powerful illustration of unwavering self-belief in action. Her ambitious goal—attempting to swim 103 miles across open ocean, without the protection of a shark cage, in her 60s—was met with widespread skepticism and even ridicule. Many considered her endeavour not only improbable but outright impossible, citing the inherent dangers posed by sharks, venomous jellyfish, unpredictable currents, and the sheer physical and mental toll of such an extreme undertaking. However, Nyad maintained an unwavering confidence in her ability to conquer this formidable challenge. This self-belief, nurtured by years of rigorous training and a deep understanding of her own physical and mental resilience, fueled her determination and allowed her to persevere through multiple failed attempts. Her eventual triumph at the age of 64 stands as a powerful testament to the transformative power of believing in oneself, even when facing seemingly insurmountable odds.

Colonel Sanders' journey to franchise his chicken recipe offers another compelling example of the importance of self-belief. Facing financial devastation in his 60s, he embarked on a demanding mission to persuade restaurant owners to adopt his unique cooking method and business model. He encountered countless rejections, often being dismissed as an aging, eccentric salesman with an improbable proposition. However, Sanders never relinquished his faith in the superior quality of his product or his ability to build a thriving business. This unwavering self-belief, deeply rooted in his understanding of his own culinary skills and his unwavering conviction in the deliciousness and marketability of his fried chicken, provided the inner strength to endure the numerous rejections and ultimately achieve remarkable success.

These narratives, and the other compelling stories within this book, demonstrate that self-belief is not simply a fleeting positive attitude; it is a fundamental driving force that empowers individuals to overcome challenges, persevere through setbacks, and ultimately transform their visions into reality. It is the unwavering inner voice that affirms "you can" even when the external world emphatically declares "you can't." This internal conviction, this deeply ingrained belief in one's own capabilities, is a crucial ingredient in the recipe for late-life achievement, enabling individuals to navigate the complexities of their journeys with unwavering confidence and resolute determination. It serves as the bedrock upon which persistence and adaptability are built, empowering individuals to transform their aspirations into tangible accomplishments.

A defining characteristic shared by the individuals who achieved remarkable feats later in life is a profound and enduring commitment to learning and growth. These were not individuals content to rest on past accomplishments or become complacent with their existing knowledge and skills. Instead, they embodied a spirit of continuous learning, constantly seeking new information, exploring innovative ideas, and diligently refining their approaches. This dedication to lifelong learning was not merely a passive accumulation of facts; it was an active and intentional pursuit of knowledge and self-improvement, a driving force that allowed them to stay ahead of the curve, adapt to changing circumstances, and continue to innovate throughout their lives. This willingness to learn and grow encompasses several key aspects.

First and foremost is a growth mindset, a belief that abilities and intelligence are not fixed traits but can be developed through dedication and hard work. This mindset fosters a love of learning, a willingness to embrace challenges, and a resilience in the face of setbacks. Individuals with a growth mindset view challenges as opportunities for growth rather than threats to their self-esteem. They are not afraid to make mistakes, as they see them as valuable learning experiences. This perspective is crucial for continuous improvement and adaptation.

Coupled with a growth mindset is a curiosity and openness to new ideas. These individuals possessed an insatiable thirst for knowledge and a genuine interest in exploring new concepts and perspectives. They were not confined by conventional thinking or established practices; they were willing to question assumptions, challenge the status quo, and embrace new ways of doing things. This openness to new ideas is essential for innovation and progress.

Furthermore, a commitment to learning and growth involves active pursuit of knowledge and skills. This may involve formal education, self-study, mentorship, or simply engaging in experiences that challenge and expand one's understanding. These individuals were not passive recipients of information; they actively sought out knowledge, engaged in experimentation, and continuously honed their skills. This proactive approach to learning allowed them to develop expertise in new areas and adapt to changing demands.

Peter Mark Roget's creation of the Thesaurus provides a compelling example of this commitment to lifelong learning. Already a distinguished physician and scientist,

Roget dedicated years to the meticulous research, organization, and categorization required to compile this comprehensive work. This undertaking required him to delve deeply into the nuances of language, exploring etymology, semantics, and the intricate relationships between words and concepts. His willingness to dedicate years of focused effort to this project, outside his primary field of expertise, demonstrates a profound commitment to learning and expanding his intellectual horizons.

Henry Ford, despite his immense success in revolutionizing automobile manufacturing, also exemplified this dedication to continuous learning. He didn't simply rest on the laurels of the Model T and the assembly line. He continued to explore new technologies, venturing into aviation and experimenting with new industrial processes. He was constantly seeking ways to improve efficiency, reduce costs, and expand his business ventures. This ongoing pursuit of knowledge and innovation allowed him to remain a dominant force in industry for decades.

These examples illustrate that a willingness to learn and grow is not a quality reserved for youth; it is a lifelong pursuit that can lead to remarkable achievements at any age. These individuals understood that learning is not a destination but a continuous journey. By embracing a growth mindset, cultivating curiosity, and actively pursuing knowledge and skills, they were able to stay ahead of the curve, adapt to changing circumstances, and continue to innovate throughout their lives. This commitment to lifelong learning is a crucial ingredient in the recipe for late-life achievement, allowing individuals to not only remain relevant but to thrive and make significant contributions to the world, regardless of their age. It demonstrates that the capacity for growth and development is not confined to a specific period of life but is a continuous potential waiting to be activated.

Many of these individuals also benefited from strong support systems. While their journeys were ultimately personal, they were often supported by family, friends, mentors, or colleagues who provided encouragement, guidance, and practical assistance. Fauja Singh's coach, Harmander Singh, played a crucial role in his marathon training. Jessica Tandy's long and successful partnership with her husband, Hume Cronyn, provided both personal and professional support. These support systems provided a foundation of strength and encouragement, helping them to navigate challenges and celebrate successes.

Perhaps the most vital thread connecting the extraordinary individuals profiled in this book is a genuine, unwavering passion for their chosen pursuits. Their driving force extended far beyond external motivations such as fame, fortune, or societal recognition. Instead, they were propelled by a deep, intrinsic love for their work, a burning inner fire that fueled their unwavering dedication and sustained them through the inevitable challenges and difficult times. This passion was not a fleeting infatuation; it was a profound connection to something larger than themselves, a source of intrinsic motivation that transformed work from a mere obligation into a deeply fulfilling and meaningful endeavour. This genuine passion manifests itself in many ways.

Firstly, it provides an intrinsic motivation that transcends external rewards. While external validation and recognition can be gratifying, they are not the primary drivers for these individuals. Their motivation stems from within, from the sheer joy and satisfaction derived from the work itself. This intrinsic motivation is far more powerful and sustainable than any external reward, providing the fuel to persevere through challenges and setbacks. When the going gets tough, it is this inner fire that keeps them going, reminding them of the deeper meaning and purpose behind their efforts.

Secondly, genuine passion fosters deep engagement and flow. When individuals are deeply passionate about their work, they often experience a state of "flow," a state of complete absorption in the task at hand. In this state, time seems to disappear, and the individual is fully present and engaged in the activity. This deep engagement not only enhances productivity and creativity but also provides a profound sense of satisfaction and fulfillment. It is in these moments of flow that individuals often produce their best work and experience the greatest sense of personal accomplishment.

Furthermore, passion cultivates resilience and perseverance. The path to achieving ambitious goals is rarely smooth. It is often filled with obstacles, setbacks, and moments of doubt. However, when individuals are driven by genuine passion, they are better equipped to weather these storms. Their deep love for their work provides the resilience to bounce back from adversity and the perseverance to keep going, even when the odds seem stacked against them. This resilience is not simply a matter of stubbornness; it is a natural by product of being deeply invested in something that truly matters to them.

Grandma Moses's paintings provide a poignant example of the power of genuine passion. Her art was not simply a way to occupy her time in her later years; it was an expression of her deep and abiding connection to rural life. Her paintings captured the beauty and simplicity of the world she knew and loved, conveying a sense of nostalgia and connection to a bygone era. This deep passion for her subject matter infused her work with a unique authenticity and emotional resonance, which is why her art continues to captivate audiences today.

Stan Lee's work in creating comic books also exemplifies the importance of genuine passion. He wasn't simply churning out stories to meet deadlines; he was passionate about telling stories that resonated with readers, sparked their imaginations, and explored universal themes of heroism, identity, and belonging. This genuine passion for storytelling infused his work with a unique energy and creativity, which is why his characters and stories have endured for generations. His work was more than just entertainment; it was a way to connect with people on a deeper level, to explore complex ideas, and to inspire hope and imagination.

These examples, among others, demonstrate that genuine passion is a crucial ingredient in the recipe for late-life achievement. It is the internal engine that drives individuals to pursue their dreams with unwavering dedication, even in the face of challenges and setbacks. It transforms work from a mere obligation into a source of deep meaning, purpose, and fulfillment. It is this unwavering passion that allows individuals to not only achieve extraordinary things but also to experience a profound sense of joy and satisfaction in the process. It is the heart and soul of their achievements, the driving force that transforms ordinary efforts into extraordinary accomplishments.

In summary, the individuals profiled in this book, while diverse in their pursuits, share a common set of qualities that distinguish them from the ordinary:

- Unwavering Persistence: A refusal to give up in the face of setbacks.

- Strong Sense of Purpose: A deep inner conviction driving their actions.
- Adaptability: The ability to adjust to changing circumstances and embrace new opportunities.
- Self-Belief: Confidence in their vision and their ability to achieve it.
- Commitment to Learning and Growth: A continuous desire to expand their knowledge and skills.
- Strong Support Systems: The presence of individuals who provide encouragement and guidance.
- Genuine Passion: A deep love for their work that fuels their dedication.

These qualities are not exclusive to these extraordinary individuals. They are qualities that we can all cultivate in our own lives. By embracing persistence, finding our purpose, adapting to change, believing in ourselves, committing to lifelong learning, building strong support systems, and pursuing our passions with genuine enthusiasm, we can all unlock our own potential and achieve extraordinary things, regardless of our age or circumstances. The stories in this book serve not just as inspiration, but as a roadmap, demonstrating that one life, lived with purpose and passion, is indeed never too late to achieve greatness.

PART THREE

Igniting Your Own Potential

17
Finding Your Fire

"The only way to do great work is to love what you do."

- Steve Jobs

The inspiring stories of individuals who achieved remarkable feats later in life serve as powerful reminders that it's never too late to pursue your dreams. But how do you begin? How do you identify the passions that lie dormant within you, waiting to be ignited? This chapter focuses on the crucial first step : finding your fire, discovering or rediscovering the passions that will fuel your journey towards a more fulfilling and purposeful life.

Many people go through life feeling a sense of unease, a nagging feeling that something is missing. They may be successful in their careers, have stable relationships, and enjoy comfortable lives, yet they still feel a lack of fulfillment. This often stems from a disconnect between their daily activities and their true passions. They may have pursued a career path based on practicality or societal expectations, neglecting the inner voice that whispers of different possibilities.

Finding your fire is a deeply personal journey of self-discovery, a process of reconnecting with the authentic self that may have become obscured by the demands and complexities of life. It's about tuning into that quiet inner voice, the one that whispers about what truly excites you, what ignites your curiosity, and what makes you feel truly alive. It's about peeling back the layers of responsibilities, self-doubt, and limiting beliefs that may have accumulated over time, burying your passions beneath a surface of routine and obligation.

This process of rediscovering your passions is not about searching for something entirely new and unfamiliar; it's often about reawakening something that has always been within you, a spark that may have dimmed over time. It's about remembering the things that truly captivated you as a child, those activities that made you lose track of time, those moments of pure joy and effortless engagement. Perhaps it was the hours spent drawing, the fascination with the intricate workings of a clock, the thrill of exploring the natural world, or the simple joy of losing yourself in a good book. These early passions, often dismissed as "childish" or "unrealistic" as we navigate the demands of adulthood, often hold valuable clues about our true calling and the activities that truly bring us joy and fulfillment.

By revisiting these early passions, we can begin to understand what truly ignites our curiosity and drives us forward. These early experiences, though seemingly insignificant, often provide a glimpse into our deepest desires and inherent talents. They offer a glimpse into the kind of work that would be not merely a job, but a source of deep satisfaction and personal fulfillment. By reconnecting with these early passions, we can begin to understand what truly matters to us, what makes us feel alive, and what we are truly capable of achieving.

This process of rediscovery is not about simply indulging in nostalgic memories; it's about using those memories as a compass, as a guide to navigate the present and chart a course for the future. It's about asking ourselves: What is it about these early passions that resonated with me so deeply? What skills and talents did I develop during those times? How can I apply those skills and passions to my life today? By exploring these questions, we can begin to bridge the gap between our childhood dreams and our current reality, allowing us to rediscover and rekindle those long-dormant passions and pursue a life that is truly aligned with our authentic selves.

Finding your fire involves self-reflection, taking time for introspection, examining your values, interests, and past experiences. It's about asking yourself honest questions about what truly matters to you, what brings you joy, and what you want to achieve in your life. This may involve journaling, meditation, or simply spending time in quiet contemplation. It also involves identifying your passions, recognizing the activities that make you feel energized, engaged, and fulfilled. These are the things that you would do even if you weren't paid for them, the things that make you lose track of time and feel truly alive. Challenging limiting beliefs is another crucial aspect, identifying and challenging the negative thoughts and self-limiting beliefs that may be holding you back. These beliefs often stem from past experiences, societal expectations, or self-doubt. Recognizing and challenging these beliefs is crucial for opening yourself up to new possibilities.

Pursuing your passions often involves stepping outside your comfort zone and taking risks, so overcoming fear and self-doubt is essential. It's important to overcome fear and self-doubt in order to pursue what truly matters to you. Finding your fire may involve trying new things, exploring different interests, and experimenting with various activities, so experimentation and exploration is key. This process of experimentation allows you to discover new passions and develop new skills. Finally, making time for the activities that ignite your fire is crucial, so creating space and time is necessary. This may involve setting boundaries with other commitments, prioritizing your passions, and creating a schedule that allows you to dedicate time to the things that matter most.

Finding your fire is not a one-time event; it's an ongoing journey of self-discovery and growth. It's about continually tuning into your inner voice, exploring your interests, and pursuing the activities that make you feel truly alive. It's about creating a life that is aligned with your authentic self and filled with purpose, passion, and joy. It's about recognizing that this fire exists within each of us, waiting to be rekindled and ignited, regardless of our age or circumstances.

This process often requires introspection and self-reflection. It's about taking the time to honestly assess your interests, values, and aspirations. It's about asking yourself some fundamental questions:

- What did I love doing as a child? Childhood passions often provide valuable clues about our true interests. What activities made you lose track of time? What brought you joy and excitement? These early passions may still hold relevance for you today.

- What am I naturally good at? Identifying your natural talents and strengths can help you pinpoint areas where you have the potential to excel. What comes easily to you? What do people compliment you on? These strengths can be valuable assets in pursuing your passions.

- What problems do I care about solving? Many people find purpose in working towards solutions to problems they care deeply about. What issues ignite your passion? What changes would you like to see in the world? These concerns can provide a powerful sense of direction.

- What activities make me feel energized and alive? Pay attention to the activities that leave you feeling invigorated and inspired. What makes you lose track of time? What brings you a sense of flow and deep engagement? These activities are likely connected to your true passions.

- If I had unlimited time and resources, what would I do? This question helps to remove the constraints of practicality and allows you to explore your deepest desires. What would you pursue if there were no limitations?

This exploration of passions requires active engagement and experimentation. Once you've started to identify potential passions – those sparks from childhood, those fleeting interests that capture your attention – it's crucial to go beyond mere introspection and take action. This phase is about turning passive contemplation into active engagement by stepping outside of your comfort zone and actively exploring these potential avenues.

Trying new things could involve anything from taking a cooking class to learning to play an instrument, joining a book club to volunteering at a local animal shelter. The key is to expose yourself to new experiences and see what resonates with you. Formal or informal classes can provide structured learning opportunities and allow you to delve deeper into a particular area of interest. Consider taking a pottery class, joining a writing workshop, or enrolling in an online course on a subject that intrigues you.

Connecting with like-minded individuals can be incredibly rewarding, so consider joining clubs, attending meetups, or participating in online communities related to your interests. Engaging with others who share your passions can provide inspiration, support, and new perspectives.

This phase of exploration is not about finding the "perfect" passion overnight. It's about experimenting, discovering what you enjoy, and gradually narrowing down your focus. Some experiences may not resonate with you, and that's okay. The process of elimination is just as valuable as the process of discovery. By actively engaging with your interests, you'll gain a deeper understanding of what truly excites you and what brings you a sense of fulfillment.

This phase requires a degree of experimentation and a willingness to step outside of your comfort zone. It's natural to feel a bit apprehensive or uncertain as you venture into the unknown. However, it's important to embrace these feelings and view them as opportunities for growth and self-discovery. Remember, the goal is not to find the "perfect" passion, but to explore your interests, discover what you love, and ultimately create a life that is fulfilling and meaningful to you.

It’s also crucial to address any limiting beliefs that may be holding you back. Many people have internalized negative messages about their abilities or their potential. They may believe they’re not talented enough, not smart enough, or not young enough to pursue their dreams. These limiting beliefs can be incredibly damaging, preventing them from even taking the first step.

Challenging these beliefs requires conscious effort. It’s about recognizing that they are just thoughts, not facts, and that you have the power to change them. It’s about focusing on your strengths and celebrating your past successes, no matter how small. It’s about surrounding yourself with supportive people who believe in you and encourage you to pursue your dreams.

Tackling Fear of Failure

Fear of failure stands as a significant obstacle, often preventing individuals from pursuing new passions, exploring uncharted territories, and ultimately realizing their full potential. This fear, deeply ingrained in many, manifests as a reluctance to try something new, a hesitation rooted in the apprehension of not succeeding. It's a fear that whispers doubts, paints worst-case scenarios, and ultimately paralyzes action. However, a crucial shift in perspective is necessary to overcome this debilitating force: recognizing failure not as a finality or a reflection of personal inadequacy, but as an integral and indispensable component of the learning process. It is through our mistakes, through our missteps and stumbles, that we truly grow, develop, and gain the wisdom necessary to achieve our goals. Embracing failure as an opportunity for learning, rather than shunning it as a source of shame, is the key to unlocking our potential and allowing ourselves to take the necessary risks for growth and achievement.

The fear of failure often stems from a fixed mindset, a belief that our abilities and intelligence are static and unchangeable. In this mindset, failure is perceived as a direct reflection of our inherent limitations, a confirmation of our inadequacy. This can lead to a fear of taking risks, a desire to avoid situations where failure is possible, and a reluctance to step outside our comfort zones. However, adopting a growth mindset, the belief that our abilities can be developed through dedication and hard work, transforms the perception of failure. In a growth mindset, failure is seen as a valuable learning opportunity, a chance to identify areas for improvement and refine our approach. It is not a judgment on our character or our inherent worth, but simply a data point on the path to mastery.

This shift in perspective is crucial for overcoming the fear of failure and embracing risk-taking. When we view failure as a learning opportunity, we become less afraid of making mistakes. We understand that mistakes are not something to be avoided at all costs, but rather valuable sources of feedback that can help us improve. This allows us to take risks, to try new things, and to push ourselves beyond our current limitations. It is in this space of discomfort, in this willingness to embrace the possibility of failure, that true growth and development occur.

Embracing Failure as a Learning Opportunity

Consciously choosing to view failure not as a negative judgment but as a valuable learning experience. This involves shifting our internal dialogue from self-criticism to self-reflection, asking questions like, "What can I learn from this?" and "How can I do better next time?"

Taking the time to carefully analyze what went wrong, identifying the specific factors that contributed to the setback. This involves being honest with ourselves about our own role in the outcome and avoiding the temptation to blame external factors.

Identifying the key lessons learned from the experience and applying them to future endeavours. This involves developing specific strategies for improvement and implementing them in a deliberate and intentional way.

Building the capacity to bounce back from setbacks and maintain a positive outlook, even in the face of adversity. This involves cultivating emotional fortitude, practicing self-compassion, and focusing on solutions rather than dwelling on the problem.

Shifting our focus from solely achieving the desired outcome to also valuing the effort, dedication, and learning that occurred along the way. This helps us to appreciate the process of growth and development, even when we don't achieve our initial goals.

The stories of many successful individuals are filled with examples of embracing failure as a stepping stone to success. Thomas Edison, for instance, famously conducted thousands of failed experiments before inventing the light bulb. He didn't view these failures as defeats; rather, he saw them as valuable lessons that brought him closer to his goal. He famously said, "I have not failed. I've just found 10,000 ways that won't work." This perspective allowed him to persevere through countless setbacks and ultimately achieve one of the most significant inventions in human history.

Similarly, J.K. Rowling, the author of the Harry Potter series, faced numerous rejections from publishers before finding success. She could have easily given up on her dream of becoming a published author after facing so much rejection. However, she persisted, believing in the power of her story and using each rejection as an opportunity to refine her work. Her eventual success is a testament to the power of embracing failure and refusing to give up on one's dreams.

These examples, and countless others, demonstrate that failure is not the opposite of success; it is a crucial part of the journey. By embracing failure as an opportunity for learning, we can overcome the fear that holds us back and unlock our true potential. This is especially important for those pursuing new passions or reinventing themselves later in life. They may face unique challenges and insecurities, but by adopting a growth mindset and embracing the possibility of failure, they can open themselves up to new experiences, new skills, and new levels of achievement.

It is in this willingness to embrace imperfection and learn from our mistakes that we discover the true meaning of growth and unlock the potential for extraordinary achievements.

Finding your fire is not a singular event; it's an ongoing process of self-discovery. Your passions may evolve over time, and that's perfectly okay. The important thing is to remain open to new experiences, to continue exploring your interests, and to stay connected to your inner voice.

Practice these exercises to help you find your fire:

- **The Passion Inventory** Create a list of everything that interests you, no matter how big or small. Don't censor yourself; just write down everything that comes to mind. Then, review your list and look for patterns or themes.

- **The Ideal Day Exercise** Imagine your ideal day. What are you doing? Who are you with? How do you feel? This exercise can help you identify the activities and experiences that bring you joy and fulfillment.

- **The Eulogy Exercise** Imagine you are at your own funeral. What would you want people to say about your life? What impact would you want to have made on the world? This exercise can help you clarify your values and priorities.

Finding your fire is the first step towards creating a more fulfilling and purposeful life. It's about reconnecting with your true passions and embracing the potential that lies within you. It's about recognizing that it's never too late to pursue your dreams and that the journey towards a more meaningful life can begin at any age. The next chapter will explore how to overcome the obstacles that may stand in your way as you pursue your newfound passions.

18

Building Your Bridge - Overcoming Obstacles

"The only way to overcome obstacles is to face them."

- Seneca

Discovering your passions is a crucial first step, but the journey towards realizing them is rarely without obstacles. This chapter focuses on "Building Your Bridge," equipping you with strategies and tools to navigate the challenges that may arise as you pursue your newfound fire. These obstacles can be internal, such as fear and self-doubt, or external, such as time constraints and lack of resources. Learning to address these challenges effectively is essential for maintaining momentum and achieving your goals.

One of the most common internal obstacles is fear. Fear of failure, fear of judgment, fear of the unknown - these anxieties can paralyze us, preventing us from even taking the first step. It's important to acknowledge that fear is a natural human emotion. It's not about eliminating fear entirely, but about learning to manage it and prevent it from controlling our actions.One effective strategy for managing fear we learnt earlier is to reframe it. Instead of viewing fear as a negative force, try to see it as a sign that you're stepping outside your comfort zone, which is essential for growth. Recognize that discomfort is often a precursor to progress.

Breaking down large, ambitious goals into smaller, more manageable steps is a highly effective strategy for overcoming feelings of overwhelm and making progress toward long-term objectives. This approach, often referred to as "chunking" or "micro-goals," transforms daunting tasks into a series of achievable milestones, making the overall journey less intimidating and significantly increasing the likelihood of success. This strategy is particularly valuable when pursuing new passions or reinventing oneself later in life, when the scope of a new endeavour can feel especially overwhelming.

Breaking Down Goals

By breaking down the larger goal into smaller, more digestible components, we shift our focus from the overwhelming end result to the achievable steps that will lead us there. This process creates a sense of order and structure, providing a clear roadmap for progress. Each smaller step becomes a mini-goal in itself, offering a sense of accomplishment upon completion and reinforcing the belief that the overall objective is attainable. This sense of progress, even in small increments, is crucial for maintaining motivation and reducing feelings of anxiety. When confronted with a task that seems vast and intricate, it's natural to feel lost, unsure of where to begin, and even paralyzed by the sheer scope of the undertaking. This sense of being overwhelmed can lead to procrastination, avoidance, and ultimately, a diminished likelihood of achieving the goal. However, by strategically dividing the overall objective into a series of smaller, achievable steps, we create a clear and actionable pathway forward, transforming a daunting challenge into a series of manageable tasks. This process not only makes the goal seem less intimidating but also significantly reduces stress and anxiety, fostering a sense of control and empowering us to make consistent progress.

The feeling of being overwhelmed often arises from focusing on the sheer magnitude of the final goal. When we fixate on the end result–writing a novel, starting a business, learning a new language–the task can seem so vast and complex that it paralyzes us into inaction. However, by breaking down this large goal into smaller, more digestible components, we create a clear pathway forward, transforming a seemingly impossible dream into a series of achievable steps.

For example, if the ultimate goal is to write a novel, the key milestones might include: completing a detailed outline, writing the first draft, revising the manuscript, and finding a publisher. Each of these milestones can then be broken down into smaller, more actionable steps. For example, the "writing the first draft" milestone could be broken down into daily or weekly word count targets, specific chapter goals, or setting aside dedicated writing time each day.

Similarly, if the goal is to learn a new language, the key milestones might include: learning the alphabet and basic pronunciation, mastering basic grammar and vocabulary, being able to hold simple conversations, and achieving fluency. Each of these milestones can then be broken down into smaller steps, such as learning a certain number of new words each week, practicing pronunciation daily, or engaging in online language exchanges.

Small Victories and Celebration

Focusing on achieving small victories along the way is crucial for building momentum and maintaining motivation. Each completed step, each achieved milestone, serves as a tangible reminder of progress and reinforces the belief that the ultimate goal is attainable. These small victories create a positive feedback loop, fuelling further effort and increasing confidence.

Celebrating each milestone, regardless of its perceived size, is a vital component of maintaining momentum and fostering sustained motivation on any journey, especially when pursuing a passion or working towards a long-term goal. Acknowledging progress and rewarding oneself for achieving these smaller goals creates a positive feedback loop, reinforcing positive habits and fuelling the desire to continue moving forward. This practice is not about throwing lavish parties for every minor accomplishment; rather, it's about cultivating a consistent habit of recognizing and appreciating the steps taken along the way.

The act of celebrating milestones serves several important psychological functions. It reinforces positive behaviour by associating positive feelings with the actions that led to the achievement. This makes it more likely that we will repeat those actions in the future, establishing positive habits and building momentum. Celebrating also boosts self-efficacy, our belief in our ability to succeed. Each time we acknowledge a milestone, we reinforce the message that we are capable of achieving our goals, which in turn increases our confidence and motivates us to take on new challenges. Furthermore, consistent acknowledgement of progress helps to combat negative self-talk and self-doubt. By focusing on what we have accomplished, we shift our attention away from perceived shortcomings and cultivate a more positive and empowering self-image. On a more practical level, celebrating milestones helps to maintain motivation throughout the often lengthy journey toward larger goals. The path to achieving significant objectives can be demanding and challenging, and celebrating smaller victories provides much-needed boosts of encouragement, reminding us of the progress we have made and fuelling our desire to continue. Finally, celebrating achievements adds a sense of enjoyment and fulfillment to the entire process. It transforms the pursuit of goals from a mere grind into a more rewarding and satisfying experience.

The form that these celebrations take can vary widely, and the most effective approach will depend on individual preferences and the specific nature of the milestone. It's crucial to understand that the celebration doesn't need to be extravagant or expensive to be effective. It could be something as simple as taking a short break to relax and recharge, indulging in a favourite activity like reading a book or listening to music, or sharing the achievement with a supportive friend or family member. The act of verbalizing the accomplishment and sharing it with someone else can provide external validation and further enhance the sense of achievement. Other simple celebrations might include enjoying a special meal, spending time in nature, or treating oneself to a small purchase. The key is not the size or cost of the reward, but the intention behind it: to acknowledge the progress made and to recognize the effort invested.

The core principle is to make the celebration meaningful and personally relevant. It should be something that genuinely acknowledges the effort and progress made, reinforcing positive habits and fuelling continued motivation. This practice is particularly beneficial when pursuing long-term goals or embarking on challenging new endeavours, as it provides regular opportunities to pause, reflect, and appreciate the journey. It is also particularly important for those embarking on new paths later in life, as it can help to build confidence and maintain enthusiasm in the face of new challenges. Consistently acknowledging progress and rewarding oneself for effort creates a positive feedback loop that propels us forward, transforming the pursuit of our goals into a more enjoyable and sustainable journey.

Self Doubt

Self-doubt, a pervasive and insidious internal obstacle, frequently hinders individuals from pursuing their aspirations and realizing their full potential. This inner critic, often manifesting as negative self-talk, constantly questions abilities, undermines confidence, and casts shadows of doubt on the possibility of success. It's a relentless internal voice that whispers insidious messages of inadequacy, telling us we're not good enough, not smart enough, not capable enough. This internal negativity can be incredibly damaging, eroding self-esteem, stifling creativity, and ultimately preventing us from taking the necessary risks to achieve our goals. Overcoming self-doubt requires conscious and sustained effort, a deliberate process of becoming aware of these negative thought patterns, challenging their validity, and actively replacing them with positive affirmations and a more constructive inner dialogue.

The origins of self-doubt are rarely simple or singular; they are typically complex and multifaceted, woven from a tapestry of contributing factors that can vary significantly from person to person. These roots often lie buried in past experiences, societal pressures, and internalized negative messages, creating a tangled web of self-perception that can significantly hinder personal growth and achievement. Understanding these roots is the first step towards effectively addressing and overcoming self-doubt.

Early childhood experiences play a crucial role in shaping our self-perception. Experiences of criticism, rejection, or lack of support during formative years can leave lasting scars, contributing to the development of negative self-images and a pervasive sense of inadequacy. Critical feedback from parents, teachers, or peers, even if well-intentioned, can be internalized as evidence of personal flaws or limitations. Similarly, experiences of failure, whether in academic pursuits, social interactions, or other endeavours, can create a fear of future failures and a belief that one is simply not capable of achieving success. These early experiences can create a foundation of self-doubt that persists into adulthood, influencing how we perceive ourselves and our abilities.

Societal pressures also contribute significantly to the development of self-doubt. Society often sets rigid standards for success, achievement, and even personal appearance, creating a constant pressure to conform. These standards, often perpetuated through media, advertising, and social interactions, can be incredibly difficult to meet, leading to feelings of inadequacy and self-doubt when individuals feel they don't measure up to these external expectations. The constant comparison to others, especially in today's hyper-connected world of social media, can further exacerbate these feelings, as individuals often compare their behind-the-scenes reality to others' carefully curated online personas. This can create a distorted perception of reality and fuel feelings of inadequacy and self-doubt.

Perhaps the most insidious source of self-doubt is the internalization of negative messages, whether they originate from external sources or from our own internal critic. When we repeatedly hear negative messages about ourselves, whether from others or from our own internal dialogue, we begin to internalize them as truths. These internalized messages become deeply ingrained beliefs that shape our self-perception and influence our behaviour. The internal critic, that inner voice that constantly judges, criticizes, and doubts our abilities, can be particularly damaging. This inner critic often uses harsh and unforgiving language, reinforcing negative self-perceptions and creating a cycle of self-doubt that becomes increasingly difficult to break.

This cycle of self-doubt can be described as negative experiences or messages which lead to negative self-perceptions, which in turn lead to negative thoughts and feelings. These negative thoughts and feelings then influence behaviour, often leading to avoidance of challenges, self-sabotage, or a reluctance to pursue opportunities. This behaviour then reinforces the initial negative self-perceptions, perpetuating the cycle. Breaking this cycle requires conscious effort and a deliberate shift in perspective. It involves challenging negative thoughts, reframing past experiences, and cultivating a more positive and supportive inner dialogue. Recognizing the complex and multifaceted roots of self-doubt is the first step towards dismantling its power and cultivating a stronger sense of self-belief.

This inner critic often employs several common tactics:

Negative Self-Talk

This involves a constant stream of negative thoughts and self-criticisms, such as "I'm not good enough," "I'll never be able to do this," or "I'm going to fail." This negative self-talk can erode confidence and create a sense of hopelessness.

Comparing Ourselves to Others

Constantly comparing ourselves to others, especially on social media, can lead to feelings of inadequacy and self-doubt. We often compare our behind-the-scenes reality to others' carefully curated highlight reels, leading to unrealistic expectations and feelings of falling short.

Focusing on Weaknesses

Obsessively focusing on our perceived weaknesses and ignoring our strengths can reinforce self-doubt. This creates a distorted view of ourselves, making us feel less capable than we actually are.

Catastrophizing

Imagining the worst possible outcomes and dwelling on potential failures can amplify fear and self-doubt. This can lead to paralysis by analysis, preventing us from taking action.

Discounting Positive Experiences

Minimizing or dismissing our accomplishments and successes can prevent us from building confidence and overcoming self-doubt. We may attribute our successes to luck or external factors, rather than recognizing our own skills and efforts.

Challenging self-doubt requires a conscious and deliberate effort to counteract these negative thought patterns. It's about becoming aware of the inner critic's tactics and actively working to dismantle its power.

What should one do.

Become Aware of Negative Thoughts

The first step is to become aware of the negative thoughts that are running through your mind. It's like turning on a light in a darkened room - suddenly, you can see what's been lurking in the shadows. These negative thoughts, often operating on autopilot, can be insidious and pervasive, undermining your confidence and hindering your progress. They might sound like "I'm not good enough," "I'm going to fail," or "I don't deserve success."

These thoughts, if left unchecked, can create a self-fulfilling prophecy, leading to inaction and missed opportunities.

Imagine this: An artist, despite years of honing their craft, finds themselves constantly plagued by thoughts like "My work isn't original," or "I'm not talented enough to succeed." These negative thoughts can paralyze them, preventing them from creating and sharing their art.

Similarly, a student preparing for an exam might be plagued by thoughts like "I'm not going to pass," or "I'm not as smart as the other students." These thoughts can create anxiety, hinder their focus, and ultimately impact their performance.

By paying attention to your internal dialogue, you can begin to identify these recurring themes of self-doubt. Notice the patterns. Do you find yourself constantly criticizing your efforts? Do you compare yourself negatively to others? Are you overly focused on avoiding failure rather than striving for success? Identifying these patterns is crucial for understanding the root causes of your self-doubt and developing strategies to address them.

This process of becoming aware of your negative thoughts requires conscious effort and a willingness to be honest with yourself. It's not always easy to confront these thoughts, as they can be deeply ingrained and often arise unconsciously. However, by shining a light on these thoughts, you can begin to challenge their validity and replace them with more positive and empowering beliefs.

Challenge the Validity of Negative Thoughts

Once you become aware of these negative thoughts – those self-doubting whispers like "I'm not good enough" or "I'm going to fail" – the next step is to critically examine them. Ask yourself: "Is there any real evidence to support this belief?" Often, these thoughts are not based on objective reality, but rather on assumptions, fears, or past experiences that may no longer be relevant.

For example, let's say an artist experiences a setback - a painting doesn't turn out as expected, or a piece of their work is rejected by a gallery. A negative thought might be: "I'm not a talented artist. I should give up." However, upon closer examination, is this truly accurate? Has this artist always failed? Have they never received positive feedback on their work before?

Similarly, a student preparing for an exam might experience the thought: "I'm going to fail this test." This thought might stem from past anxieties about exams or a single poor performance. However, is it necessarily true? Have they consistently failed exams in the past? Have they adequately prepared for this particular exam?

By questioning these negative thoughts and seeking evidence to support or refute them, we can begin to dismantle their power. We can start to see that these thoughts are often based on assumptions, generalizations, or past experiences that may not accurately reflect our current abilities or the present situation.

This process of challenging negative thoughts requires a degree of self-awareness and a willingness to question our own assumptions. It's helpful to consider alternative explanations for the situation and to focus on evidence that contradicts the negative thought. By systematically challenging these negative beliefs, we can begin to break free from their grip and cultivate a more positive and empowering inner dialogue.

Replace Negative Thoughts with Positive Affirmations

Once you become aware of these negative thoughts - those self-doubting whispers like "I'm not good enough" or "I'm going to fail" - the next crucial step is to critically examine them. Ask yourself: "Is there any real evidence to support this belief?" Often, these thoughts are not based on objective reality, but rather on assumptions, fears, or past experiences that may no longer be relevant.

For example, let's say an artist experiences a setback - a painting doesn't turn out as expected, or a piece of their work is rejected by a gallery. A negative thought might immediately arise: "I'm not a talented artist. I should give up." This thought, fuelled by disappointment and frustration, might seem valid in the moment. However, upon closer examination, is it truly accurate? Has this artist always failed? Have they never received positive feedback on their work before? Have they considered the possibility that this particular piece might not have resonated with the specific gallery or that the feedback received might offer valuable insights for future creations?

Similarly, a student preparing for an exam might be plagued by the thought: "I'm going to fail this test." This thought might stem from past anxieties about exams or a single poor performance in the past. However, is it necessarily true in this specific instance? Have they adequately prepared for this particular exam? Have they identified their strengths and weaknesses and developed strategies to address any areas of concern?

By questioning these negative thoughts and seeking evidence to support or refute them, we can begin to dismantle their power. We can start to see that these thoughts are often based on assumptions, generalizations, or past experiences that may not accurately reflect our current abilities or the present situation. This process of challenging negative thoughts requires a degree of self-awareness and a willingness to question our own assumptions. It's helpful to consider alternative explanations for the situation and to focus on evidence that contradicts the negative thought. By systematically challenging these negative beliefs, we can begin to break free from their grip and cultivate a more positive and empowering inner dialogue.

Focus on Your Strengths and Past Successes

Once you become aware of these negative thoughts - those self-doubting whispers like "I'm not good enough" or "I'm going to fail" - the next crucial step is to critically examine them. Ask yourself: "Is there any real evidence to support this belief?" Often, these thoughts are not based on objective reality, but rather on assumptions, fears, or past experiences that may no longer be relevant.

For example, let's say an artist experiences a setback - a painting doesn't turn out as expected, or a piece of their work is rejected by a gallery. A negative thought might immediately arise: "I'm not a talented artist. I should give up." This thought, fuelled by disappointment and frustration, might seem valid in the moment. However, upon closer examination, is it truly accurate? Has this artist always failed? Have they never received positive feedback on their work before? Have they considered the possibility that this particular piece might not have resonated with the specific gallery or that the feedback received might offer valuable insights for future creations?

Similarly, a student preparing for an exam might be plagued by the thought: "I'm going to fail this test." This thought might stem from past anxieties about exams or a single poor performance in the past. However, is it necessarily true in this specific instance? Have they adequately prepared for this particular exam? Have they identified their strengths and weaknesses and developed strategies to address any areas of concern?

By questioning these negative thoughts and seeking evidence to support or refute them, we can begin to dismantle their power. We can start to see that these thoughts are often based on assumptions, generalizations, or past experiences that may not accurately reflect our current abilities or the present situation. This process of challenging negative thoughts requires a degree of self-awareness and a willingness to question our own assumptions. It's helpful to consider alternative explanations for the situation and to focus on evidence that contradicts the negative thought. By systematically challenging these negative beliefs, we can begin to break free from their grip and cultivate a more positive and empowering inner dialogue.

Practice Self-Compassion

Just as you would offer a helping hand and words of encouragement to a friend facing a challenge, it's crucial to extend that same level of kindness and understanding towards yourself. When you make a mistake, stumble, or face a setback, treat yourself with the same compassion and understanding you would offer a dear friend.

Imagine a friend confides in you about a failed project or a difficult experience. How would you respond? Would you criticize them harshly, or would you offer words of support and encouragement? You would likely offer them words of comfort, remind them of their past successes, and emphasize the valuable lessons learned from the experience.

Similarly, when faced with a setback, treat yourself with the same kindness and understanding. Acknowledge your feelings, but avoid self-criticism. Instead of dwelling on the negative, focus on the lessons learned and the steps you can take to improve. Remind yourself of your past successes, your strengths, and your resilience. Celebrate your efforts and acknowledge the courage it takes to step outside your comfort zone and try new things.

By cultivating self-compassion, you create a supportive inner environment that fosters growth and resilience. This doesn't mean being overly indulgent or avoiding accountability, but rather recognizing that everyone makes mistakes and that these experiences are opportunities for learning and growth. By treating yourself with kindness and understanding, you cultivate a more positive and supportive inner dialogue, paving the way for greater self-acceptance and a more fulfilling journey of personal growth.

Surround Yourself with Supportive People

Surrounding yourself with supportive people is crucial in navigating life's challenges and pursuing your passions. These individuals act as a sounding board, offering encouragement, and providing a safe space for growth and self-discovery.

Imagine an aspiring writer struggling with self-doubt. They might find solace in a supportive writing group where members share their work, offer constructive criticism, and celebrate each other's successes. The encouragement and camaraderie within this group can significantly boost their confidence and motivate them to continue writing.

Similarly, an entrepreneur launching a new business might benefit immensely from a network of mentors, advisors, and fellow entrepreneurs who offer guidance, share their experiences, and provide a sounding board for their ideas. These connections can provide invaluable support, helping the entrepreneur navigate challenges, overcome obstacles, and stay motivated on their journey.

Beyond professional support, personal relationships also play a vital role. Friends and family members who believe in you, celebrate your accomplishments, and offer a listening ear can significantly impact your self-esteem and resilience. They can provide a much-needed emotional buffer during challenging times and offer a different perspective on your goals and aspirations.

Cultivating a supportive network requires conscious effort. It involves seeking out individuals who share your values and interests, building genuine connections, and actively nurturing these relationships. It's about finding people who uplift you, challenge you to grow, and celebrate your successes. By surrounding yourself with individuals who believe in you and encourage your dreams, you create a positive and supportive environment that fosters personal growth and empowers you to achieve your full potential.

Take Action Despite Fear

Once you've become aware of the negative thoughts that tend to creep into your mind - those self-doubting whispers like "I'm not good enough" or "I'm going to fail" - it's crucial to actively counter them with positive affirmations. This involves consciously shifting your internal dialogue from a critical, self-deprecating tone to one of encouragement and self-support.

Imagine an athlete preparing for a competition. Negative thoughts might include, "I'm not strong enough," or "I'm going to lose." Instead of dwelling on these anxieties, the athlete can consciously replace them with positive affirmations such as, "I have trained diligently for this," or "I am strong and capable." This shift in internal dialogue can significantly impact their performance, boosting their confidence and focus.

Similarly, a writer struggling with a creative block might find themselves plagued by thoughts like, "My writing is terrible," or "I'm not a talented writer." Instead of succumbing to these negative thoughts, they can consciously replace them with affirmations such as, "I have unique perspectives and stories to share," or "I am a writer, and I will continue to write." These affirmations not only counter the negative self-talk but also remind the writer of their strengths and their commitment to their craft.

This process of replacing negative thoughts with positive affirmations requires consistent practice. It may feel awkward or even insincere at first, but with persistent effort, it can become a more natural and automatic response. By consciously cultivating a more positive and supportive inner dialogue, you can create a more empowering internal environment that fosters self-belief, resilience, and a greater sense of self-worth. This inner shift can have a profound impact on your motivation, your actions, and ultimately, your ability to achieve your goals.

External obstacles, those challenges originating from outside ourselves, can significantly impede the pursuit of new passions and goals, particularly later in life when existing responsibilities often accumulate. Among these external obstacles, time constraints stand out as a particularly common and pervasive concern. Individuals juggling existing commitments such as full-time jobs, family responsibilities, caregiving duties, community involvement, or other obligations often find themselves struggling to carve out the necessary time to explore new interests or embark on new ventures. The feeling that there simply aren't enough hours in the day can create a sense of frustration, discouragement, and even resignation, leading many to believe that pursuing their passions is simply impossible.

Time Constraints

This feeling of being perpetually time-constrained is often exacerbated by several factors:

Existing Responsibilities Individuals in later life often have a complex web of existing responsibilities. They may be caring for aging parents, raising grandchildren, maintaining a household, or managing ongoing health concerns. These responsibilities can consume a significant amount of time and energy, leaving little room for new pursuits.

Lack of Flexibilit Many individuals have limited flexibility in their schedules due to work commitments, family obligations, or other fixed appointments. This lack of flexibility can make it difficult to schedule dedicated time for pursuing new passions.

Perception of Time as a Scarce Resource The perception that time is a limited and dwindling resource can create a sense of urgency and pressure, making it difficult to prioritize new activities. This can lead to a feeling that there simply isn't enough time to do everything, leading to procrastination or abandonment of new goals.

Difficulty Setting Boundaries Setting boundaries between existing responsibilities and new pursuits can be challenging. Individuals may feel obligated to prioritize others' needs over their own, leading to a constant struggle to find time for themselves.

However, while time constraints are a real and valid challenge, they are not insurmountable. Several strategies can be employed to effectively manage time and create space for pursuing new passions:

Prioritization

Identifying the most important tasks and focusing on those first. This involves evaluating existing commitments and determining which ones are truly essential and which ones can be delegated, reduced, or eliminated.

Scheduling

Creating a realistic schedule that allocates specific time slots for pursuing new passions. This involves treating these time slots as important appointments that should not be easily canceled or rescheduled.

Time Blocking

Dividing the day into specific blocks of time dedicated to different activities. This helps to create structure and accountability, making it easier to stay focused and avoid distractions.

Micro-Moments

Utilizing small pockets of time throughout the day to make progress on goals. Even dedicating 15-30 minutes each day can accumulate to significant progress over time.

Delegation

Delegating tasks to others whenever possible. This can free up valuable time and energy that can be dedicated to pursuing new passions.

Saying No

Learning to say no to new commitments or requests that would further strain available time. This involves setting boundaries and prioritizing personal well-being.

Combining Activities

Finding ways to combine existing responsibilities with new pursuits. For example, listening to audiobooks or podcasts while commuting or exercising.

Re-evaluating Existing Routines

Examining current daily and weekly routines to identify areas where time can be more efficiently utilized. This may involve streamlining tasks, eliminating time-wasting activities, or adjusting schedules.

Effectively managing time constraints is not about magically creating more hours in the day; it's about making the most of the time available. By prioritizing tasks, scheduling dedicated time, utilizing micro-moments, and setting appropriate boundaries, individuals can create the space they need to pursue their passions, even within the context of existing responsibilities. This proactive approach to time management transforms the perception of time from a scarce and limiting resource to a manageable and valuable asset, empowering individuals to pursue their dreams and enrich their lives, regardless of their current circumstances. This is especially important for those embarking on new endeavours later in life, as effective time management allows them to integrate new passions seamlessly into their existing routines and create a fulfilling and balanced life.

Effective time management is paramount for navigating the challenge of time constraints, particularly for individuals juggling existing responsibilities while aspiring to pursue new passions. It's not about magically creating more hours in the day, but rather about maximizing the value of the time available and strategically allocating it to the most important activities. This involves a conscious and deliberate approach to prioritizing tasks, setting realistic goals, and creating a structured schedule that integrates new pursuits seamlessly into existing routines. Even dedicating small, consistent amounts of time each day or week can accumulate into significant progress over time, demonstrating the power of consistent effort and strategic planning.

Effective time management is not about striving for perfect efficiency; it's about creating a sustainable and balanced approach that allows for both productivity and personal fulfillment. It's about recognizing that time is a valuable resource and making conscious choices about how it is spent. By implementing these strategies, individuals can create the space they need to pursue their passions, enrich their lives, and achieve their goals, regardless of their existing responsibilities or time constraints. This proactive approach empowers individuals to not just manage their time, but to master it, transforming the perception of time from a limiting factor to a powerful tool for achieving their dreams.

Lack of Resources

A significant external obstacle that can hinder the pursuit of new passions and goals, especially later in life, is a perceived or actual lack of resources. This scarcity can manifest in various forms: financial limitations, lack of access to necessary materials or equipment, or a limited social network or support system. This perceived lack can create a feeling of being ill-equipped, making the pursuit of dreams seem unattainable and fostering a sense of discouragement. However, it's crucial to recognize that resourcefulness–the ability to find creative solutions and make the most of available resources–can often compensate for a lack of abundance. Resourcefulness is not about having everything you need; it's about finding ways to achieve your goals with what you have.

This perceived lack of resources can manifest in several ways:

Financial Constraints

Limited financial resources can make it difficult to afford necessary equipment, materials, training, or other expenses associated with pursuing a new passion. This can be particularly challenging for those on fixed incomes or facing financial hardship.

Lack of Access to Materials or Equipment

Pursuing certain passions may require specialized equipment, materials, or facilities that are not readily accessible. This can create a significant barrier, especially for those living in remote areas or lacking access to transportation.

Limited Social Network or Support System

A lack of connections within a particular field or a limited social network can make it difficult to find mentors, collaborators, or other forms of support. This can lead to feelings of isolation and make it more challenging to navigate the complexities of pursuing a new path.

Lack of Information or Knowledge

Not knowing where to start, what resources are available, or how to navigate a particular field can create a sense of being ill-prepared. This lack of information can be particularly daunting for those venturing into unfamiliar territory.

However, resourcefulness can be a powerful antidote to these challenges. How can one do it. Embrace these methods.

Creative Problem-Solving

Resourceful individuals are adept at finding creative solutions to overcome obstacles. They are able to think outside the box, identify alternative approaches, and make the most of limited resources.

Networking and Collaboration

Building connections with others in the field can provide access to valuable resources, information, and support. Networking can open doors to opportunities that might not have been otherwise accessible.

Utilizing Free or Low-Cost Resources

Many free or low-cost resources are available, such as online courses, community workshops, library resources, and open-source software. Resourceful individuals are able to identify and utilize these resources effectively.

Bartering and Trading

Exchanging skills or services with others can be a valuable way to access resources without spending money. This can involve trading skills, such as web design for marketing services, or bartering for materials or equipment.

Seeking Mentorship and Guidance

Connecting with experienced individuals in the field can provide valuable insights, advice, and support. Mentors can offer guidance on navigating challenges, accessing resources, and developing skills.

Adapting and Improvising

Being able to adapt existing resources or improvise with available materials can be crucial for overcoming limitations. This involves thinking creatively about how existing resources can be used in new and innovative ways.

For example, someone interested in learning photography but lacking the funds for expensive equipment might utilize free online tutorials, practice with a smartphone camera, or join a local photography club to learn from experienced photographers. Someone interested in starting a business but lacking funding might explore bootstrapping strategies, seek out microloans, or participate in business plan competitions.

These examples illustrate that a lack of resources does not have to be a barrier to achieving one's goals. Resourcefulness, combined with creativity, perseverance, and a willingness to seek out opportunities, can often bridge the gap between limited resources and ambitious aspirations. It's about focusing on what is available rather than dwelling on what is lacking, and finding innovative ways to make the most of existing resources. This mindset is particularly crucial for those embarking on new paths later in life, as it empowers them to pursue their passions and achieve their goals, regardless of their current circumstances. By cultivating resourcefulness, individuals can transform limitations into opportunities, turning perceived disadvantages into catalysts for creativity and innovation.

Explore creative solutions, look for free or low-cost resources, and network with others who share your interests. You may be surprised by the opportunities that exist if you're willing to be resourceful and persistent. Building a strong support system is also essential for overcoming obstacles. This involves connecting with people who share your passions, who understand your challenges, and who can provide encouragement and support along the way. Your support system can be a source of motivation, inspiration, and practical assistance.

Overcoming obstacles is an integral part of the journey towards achieving your goals. By developing effective strategies for managing fear, self-doubt, time constraints, and other challenges, you can build a strong bridge that will carry you towards your desired destination. Remember that resilience, persistence, and a positive mindset are key to navigating the inevitable bumps in the road. The next chapter will focus on taking the first steps and maintaining momentum on your journey.

19

Taking the Leap: Embracing Action and Momentum

"Leap and the net will appear."

- John Burroughs

Finding your fire and building your bridge are essential preparatory steps, but the true transformation comes from taking action. This chapter, "Taking the Leap," focuses on the crucial act of initiating your journey and maintaining momentum along the way. It's about translating your passions and plans into tangible steps, overcoming inertia, and cultivating the habits that will propel you towards your goals.

One of the biggest hurdles many people face is simply getting started. The initial leap can feel daunting, especially when pursuing a long-term goal or a significant life change. It's easy to get caught up in planning and preparation, but without taking action, your dreams will remain just that - dreams.

The key to overcoming this inertia is to focus on taking small, manageable steps. Instead of trying to tackle everything at once, break down your goals into smaller, more achievable tasks. This can make the overall objective seem less overwhelming and increase your chances of success.

For example, if your goal is to write a book, don't focus on writing the entire manuscript at once. Instead, set a daily or weekly word count target. Even writing just a few hundred words each day can accumulate into a substantial amount of progress over time.

Similarly, if you want to learn a new skill, don't try to master it overnight. Start with the basics, practice regularly, and gradually increase the complexity of your tasks. Consistent, small actions are far more effective than sporadic bursts of effort.

Once you've taken the first step towards pursuing your passion, maintaining consistent momentum becomes crucial. It's easy to get caught up in the initial excitement and motivation, but sustaining that enthusiasm over the long term can be challenging. Life often throws curveballs - unexpected obstacles, distractions, and setbacks - that can easily derail our progress.

One effective strategy for maintaining momentum is to create a consistent routine. This involves setting aside specific times each day or week for working towards your goals. For example, if you're learning to play guitar, schedule a dedicated practice session for 30 minutes each evening. If you're writing a novel, aim to write for at least an hour every morning. By establishing a regular schedule, you create a sense of structure and accountability. These dedicated time slots become non-negotiable, making it easier to stay focused and avoid procrastination.

Furthermore, a consistent routine can help to minimize the impact of distractions. When you know that a specific time is reserved for your passion, it becomes easier to resist the urge to succumb to distractions like social media, television, or other time-consuming activities. This structure provides a framework for consistent progress, even when motivation may be waning.

For example, an aspiring writer might schedule a writing session each morning before checking email or engaging with social media. This creates a dedicated block of time for focused writing, minimizing distractions and allowing them to dive deep into their creative work. Similarly, a musician might schedule daily practice sessions at the same time each day, creating a consistent rhythm that reinforces their commitment to their musical pursuits.

By establishing a consistent routine, you make the pursuit of your passions a regular part of your daily life. This not only increases your chances of success but also provides a sense of accomplishment and reinforces the positive habits that will help you achieve your goals.

Tracking your progress is also crucial for maintaining momentum. This can involve keeping a journal, using a progress tracking app, or simply marking off completed tasks on a to-do list. Visualizing your progress can provide a powerful sense of motivation and reinforce your commitment to your goals.

Maintaining momentum is crucial for achieving any goal, especially when pursuing passions later in life. It's easy to get excited at the beginning, fueled by initial enthusiasm, but sustaining that energy over the long term can be challenging. Life throws curveballs – unexpected obstacles, distractions, and setbacks – that can easily derail our progress.

One effective strategy for maintaining momentum is to create a consistent routine. This involves setting aside specific times each day or week for working towards your goals. For example, if you're learning to play the piano, schedule a dedicated practice session for 30 minutes each evening. If you're writing a novel, aim to write for at least an hour every morning. By establishing a regular schedule, you create a sense of structure and accountability. These dedicated time slots become non-negotiable, making it easier to stay focused and avoid procrastination.

Imagine a retiree who dreams of painting. By scheduling a dedicated painting session every morning after breakfast, they create a consistent routine that reinforces their commitment to their artistic pursuits. This routine not only provides dedicated time for painting but also helps to establish a sense of discipline and consistency.

Furthermore, a consistent routine can help to minimize the impact of distractions. When you know that a specific time is reserved for your passion, it becomes easier to resist the urge to succumb to distractions like social media, television, or other time-consuming activities. This structure provides a framework for consistent progress, even when motivation may be waning.

For example, a writer might schedule a writing session each morning before checking email or engaging with social media. This creates a dedicated block of time for focused writing, minimizing distractions and allowing them to dive deep into their creative work. Similarly, a musician might schedule daily practice sessions at the same time each day, creating a consistent rhythm that reinforces their commitment to their musical pursuits.

By establishing a consistent routine, you make the pursuit of your passions a regular part of your daily life. This not only increases your chances of success but also provides a sense of accomplishment and reinforces the positive habits that will help you achieve your goals.

This consistent action, even in small increments, builds momentum. It's like a snowball rolling down a hill - the more it rolls, the bigger it gets. Each small step, each consistent effort, contributes to a growing sense of momentum, making it easier to continue moving forward, even when faced with challenges.

Celebration is Important

Celebrating achievements, regardless of their perceived size, forms a crucial pillar in maintaining momentum and fostering sustained motivation. Acknowledging progress and rewarding oneself for effort reinforces positive habits, strengthens self-efficacy, and cultivates a sense of accomplishment that fuels continued forward movement. This practice is not about indulging in grand celebrations for every minor task; rather, it's about cultivating a consistent habit of recognizing and appreciating the steps taken toward larger goals, fostering a positive feedback loop that encourages further progress.

When we acknowledge and reward ourselves for completing a task or achieving a milestone, we reinforce the behaviour that led to that success. This makes it more likely that we will repeat that behaviour in the future, creating positive habits and building momentum.

Celebrating achievements, even small ones, strengthens our belief in our ability to succeed (self-efficacy). This increased self-belief makes us more likely to take on new challenges and persevere through difficulties. Regularly acknowledging accomplishments helps to counteract negative self-talk and self-doubt. By focusing on what we have achieved, we shift our attention away from perceived shortcomings and cultivate a more positive self-image. The journey toward long-term goals can be challenging and demanding. Celebrating milestones along the way provides a much-needed boost of motivation, reminding us of the progress we have made and fuelling our desire to continue moving forward. Celebrating achievements adds a sense of joy and fulfillment to the process of pursuing our goals. It transforms the journey from a mere grind into a more enjoyable and rewarding experience.

The act of celebrating can take many forms, and the most effective approach will vary depending on individual preferences and the nature of the achievement. It's not about extravagant displays or expensive rewards; it's about finding ways to acknowledge progress in a meaningful and personally relevant way. Some examples include:

Verbal Acknowledgement

Simply taking a moment to acknowledge the accomplishment and express pride in oneself can be a powerful form of celebration. This can involve saying to yourself, "I did it!" or "I'm proud of myself for completing this."

Small Rewards

Treating oneself to a small reward, such as a favourite beverage, a relaxing activity, or a small purchase, can reinforce positive behaviour and provide a tangible reminder of the achievement.

Sharing with Others

Sharing accomplishments with supportive friends, family members, or mentors can provide external validation and further enhance the sense of accomplishment.

Tracking Progress

Keeping a record of progress, such as a journal, a checklist, or a visual progress tracker, can provide a tangible reminder of how far one has come. Reviewing this progress can be a powerful source of motivation and encouragement.

Taking a Break and Reflecting

Taking some time to reflect on the accomplishment and appreciate the effort involved can be a valuable form of celebration. This can involve taking a short break, engaging in a relaxing activity, or simply taking a few moments to appreciate the progress made.

The key is to make the celebration meaningful and personally relevant. It should be something that genuinely acknowledges the effort and progress made, reinforcing positive habits and fuelling continued motivation.This practice is particularly important for those embarking on new endeavours later in life. They may be facing unique challenges and insecurities, and celebrating small victories can provide a much-needed boost of confidence and motivation. It can also help to counteract negative self-talk and reinforce the belief that they are capable of achieving their goals, regardless of their age or past experiences. By consistently acknowledging progress and rewarding themselves for their efforts, individuals can create a positive feedback loop that propels them forward on their journey towards achieving their dreams. It transforms the pursuit of goals from a daunting uphill climb into a more manageable and enjoyable journey, marked by regular milestones of accomplishment and a consistent sense of forward momentum.

Cultivating a growth mindset is paramount for navigating the challenges and embracing the opportunities inherent in pursuing personal growth and achieving meaningful goals, especially later in life. This mindset, as opposed to a fixed mindset, centers on the belief that abilities and intelligence are not static, innate qualities but rather dynamic attributes that can be developed and enhanced through dedication, effort, and perseverance. Adopting a growth mindset fundamentally alters one's relationship with learning, challenges, and setbacks, transforming them from sources of fear and avoidance into catalysts for growth and development. It fosters a love of learning, a resilience in the face of adversity, and a proactive approach to self-improvement.

A fixed mindset, on the other hand, operates on the premise that abilities and intelligence are fixed traits, predetermined and unchangeable. Individuals with a fixed mindset tend to view challenges as threats to their self-worth, avoiding situations where they might appear incompetent or make mistakes. They often interpret setbacks as evidence of their inherent limitations, leading to discouragement and a reluctance to persevere. This mindset can create a self-fulfilling prophecy, limiting potential and hindering growth.

The core difference between these two mindsets lies in their interpretation of effort and challenges. In a fixed mindset, effort is often seen as evidence of low ability. If you have to work hard at something, it implies you're not naturally good at it. Challenges are perceived as threats to self-esteem, as they expose potential weaknesses. In contrast, a growth mindset views effort as the path to mastery. Hard work is seen as essential for developing skills and abilities. Challenges are embraced as opportunities for learning and growth, providing valuable feedback and pushing individuals beyond their comfort zones.

Embracing a growth mindset has profound implications for how we approach learning, challenges, and setbacks. Individuals with a growth mindset view challenges as opportunities to stretch their abilities and learn new skills. They are not afraid of difficult tasks; instead, they see them as opportunities for growth and development. This willingness to embrace challenges is crucial for pushing beyond current limitations and achieving new levels of mastery.

In a growth mindset, mistakes are not seen as failures but as valuable learning experiences. They provide feedback that can be used to refine strategies and improve performance. Individuals with a growth mindset are not afraid to make mistakes; they see them as an essential part of the learning process. This allows them to learn from their experiences and continuously improve.

Setbacks are inevitable on any journey toward a meaningful goal. However, individuals with a growth mindset are better equipped to handle these setbacks. They view them not as evidence of their inadequacy but as temporary obstacles to be overcome. They possess greater resilience and are more likely to persevere in the face of adversity.

In a fixed mindset, the success of others can be perceived as a threat, triggering feelings of envy or insecurity. However, in a growth mindset, the success of others is seen as a source of inspiration and motivation. Individuals with a growth mindset are able to learn from the experiences of others and use their success as a catalyst for their own growth.

A growth mindset emphasizes the importance of effort and dedication in developing abilities. Individuals with this mindset understand that hard work is essential for achieving mastery and are willing to put in the necessary time and effort to improve.

Setbacks are bound to happen in any journey, especially when pursuing ambitious goals or venturing into new territory. It is not the occurrence of setbacks that defines us, but rather how we respond to them. Viewing setbacks not as failures but as opportunities for learning and growth is a hallmark of a growth mindset. This involves a conscious effort to analyze what went wrong, identify areas for improvement, and use these experiences to refine our approach.

Learning from Setbacks

Acknowledge and Accept the Setback

The first step is to acknowledge and accept that a setback has occurred. This involves resisting the temptation to deny, minimize, or blame external factors.

Analyse What Went Wrong

Carefully analyse the situation to understand the factors that contributed to the setback. This involves being honest with oneself and identifying areas where improvements can be made.

Extract Lessons Learned

Identify the key lessons learned from the experience. What can be done differently next time? What new skills or knowledge can be acquired to prevent similar setbacks in the future?

Adjust Your Approach

Use the lessons learned to refine your approach and develop new strategies. This involves adapting existing methods, experimenting with new techniques, and seeking feedback from others.

Maintain a Positive Outlook

It's important to maintain a positive outlook and avoid dwelling on negative emotions. Focus on the lessons learned and the opportunities for growth that the setback has provided.

By cultivating a growth mindset and viewing setbacks as opportunities for learning, individuals can transform challenges into catalysts for growth and development.

This is especially important for those pursuing new passions or reinventing themselves later in life. They may face unique challenges and insecurities, but by embracing a growth mindset, they can overcome these obstacles and achieve remarkable things. This shift in perspective empowers individuals to not only achieve their goals but to continuously evolve and grow throughout their lives, transforming setbacks into stepping stones on the path to success.

Some practical strategies for taking the leap and maintaining momentum:

- Start Small: Focus on taking small, manageable steps. Don't try to do everything at once.
- Create a Routine: Establish a consistent schedule for working towards your goals.
- Track Your Progress: Monitor your progress and celebrate your achievements.
- Cultivate a Growth Mindset: Believe that your abilities can be developed through effort and dedication.
- Embrace Setbacks as Learning Opportunities: View setbacks as opportunities for growth and improvement.
- Find an Accountability Partner: Connect with someone who shares your goals or who can provide support and encouragement.

- Visualize Your Success: Imagine yourself achieving your goals. This can help to strengthen your motivation and commitment.
- Be Patient and Persistent: Achieving meaningful goals takes time and effort. Be patient with yourself and persistent in your pursuit.

Taking the leap and maintaining momentum are essential for transforming your dreams into reality. By focusing on small steps, creating a routine, tracking your progress, and embracing a growth mindset, you can cultivate the habits that will propel you towards your goals. Remember that the journey is just as important as the destination. Embrace the process, celebrate your progress, and enjoy the satisfaction of knowing that you're taking action towards creating a more fulfilling and purposeful life. This final chapter brings together the themes of the book, reinforcing the core message: One life is indeed never too late to find your fire, build your bridge, and take the leap toward a more meaningful existence.

Conclusion
The Unfolding Canvas of Life

The stories within these pages, spanning diverse fields and decades of life, converge on a single, powerful truth: it is never too late. Never too late to discover a hidden passion, to pursue a long-held dream, to reinvent oneself, or to leave a lasting impact on the world. From Ray Kroc's late-life creation of a fast-food empire to Diana Nyad's triumphant swim across the Florida Straits at 64, from Grandma Moses's vibrant canvases painted in her 70s to Betty White's enduring comedic reign that spanned nearly a century, these individuals have defied conventional wisdom and redefined the narrative of aging. They have shown us that life is not a linear trajectory with a predetermined peak, but rather an unfolding canvas, constantly offering new opportunities for growth, discovery, and achievement.

We began this exploration by examining the pervasive societal pressures that contribute to the creation and perpetuation of "The Time Trap." This insidious concept represents the deeply ingrained belief that there exists a "right" time for everything in life—a narrow, often culturally defined, window of opportunity for achieving key milestones such as education, career establishment, marriage, family, and even personal fulfillment. This societal clock dictates an often rigid timeline, suggesting that certain achievements must occur within a specific age range, typically during youth and young adulthood, or they are somehow deemed less valid, less significant, or even unattainable. This "Time Trap" dictates that career changes after a certain age are risky, that pursuing a passion later in life is impractical, and that significant personal growth is largely confined to earlier stages of life.

This societal pressure to adhere to a preordained timeline is reinforced through various channels. Media portrayals often celebrate youthful success, showcasing young entrepreneurs, prodigies, and overnight sensations, further solidifying the idea that the prime years for achievement are limited to youth. Social media platforms, as discussed previously, contribute to this pressure by presenting curated highlight reels of seemingly perfect lives, often showcasing individuals achieving traditional milestones at a young age. This constant exposure to idealized and often age-centric narratives can create a sense of urgency and anxiety, leading individuals to believe they are falling behind if their lives don't mirror these carefully constructed portrayals.

The "Time Trap" exerts a powerful influence on our self-perception, leading to the development of self-limiting beliefs. These beliefs, often internalized from societal messages and external pressures, create mental barriers that prevent individuals from pursuing their passions or taking risks later in life. They manifest as internal dialogues filled with phrases like "I'm too old to start something new, "I've missed my chance," or "It's too late for me." These self-defeating thoughts erode confidence, stifle creativity, and ultimately prevent individuals from exploring their full potential. The fear of being judged, the apprehension of appearing foolish, and the internalized belief that they are no longer capable of achieving significant things can paralyze individuals, keeping them trapped within the confines of their comfort zones.

This mindset can be particularly damaging for older individuals who are considering pursuing new goals or reinventing themselves. They may feel a profound sense of being "out of time," believing that their opportunity for success has passed. They may be hesitant to invest time, energy, and resources into new ventures, fearing that they lack the energy, adaptability, or cognitive capacity to compete with younger individuals. This internalized ageism can lead to missed opportunities, unfulfilled potential, and a diminished sense of purpose.

However, the stories we've encountered throughout this book serve as powerful counter-narratives, shattering the myth of the "Time Trap" and demonstrating that the human spirit is not bound by arbitrary timelines. The individuals we've explored—from Grandma Moses picking up a paintbrush in her late 70s to Diana Nyad conquering the Florida Straits in her 60s—have defied conventional wisdom and proven that achievement, growth, and fulfillment are not limited by age. They demonstrate that the timeline we've been told to follow is not only arbitrary but profoundly limiting, a social construct that fails to capture the dynamic and evolving nature of human potential.

These stories offer compelling evidence that potential doesn't expire. They prove that passion can ignite at any age, fuelled by life experience, accumulated wisdom, and a renewed sense of purpose. They demonstrate that the pursuit of our dreams, regardless of when we begin, can lead to extraordinary outcomes, enriching not only our own lives but also the lives of those around us. These narratives provide hope and inspiration, reminding us that it's never too late to pursue our passions, embrace new challenges, and make our unique mark on the world. They reveal that the human capacity for growth, learning, and achievement is a lifelong journey, not a sprint with a predetermined finish line.

We turned our attention to the often-underestimated advantages that come with experience, recognizing that the passage of time is not simply a process of decline but also a period of profound growth and development. This exploration revealed the immense value of accumulated wisdom, resilience, self-knowledge, and crystallized intelligence–qualities honed over a lifetime of navigating both challenges and triumphs. These attributes, often overlooked in a society that tends to prioritize youth, provide a rich and fertile foundation for significant achievements later in life. They offer a unique perspective, a deeper understanding of oneself and the world, and the emotional fortitude necessary to persevere through difficulties, all of which are invaluable assets when pursuing new endeavours or reinventing oneself.

Let's delve deeper into these key advantages. Life experience provides a wealth of knowledge and insights that cannot be gained through formal education or theoretical study alone. This accumulated wisdom encompasses a broad range of experiences, including successes, failures, relationships, personal growth, and navigating various life stages. This wisdom provides a deeper understanding of human nature, societal dynamics, and the complexities of the world, offering a valuable perspective when making decisions, solving problems, and pursuing goals. It's the kind of knowledge that comes from having "been there, done that," offering a nuanced understanding of potential pitfalls and effective strategies.

As discussed previously, life inevitably presents challenges and setbacks. Each challenge overcome strengthens our resilience, our ability to bounce back from adversity. This resilience, built over time through navigating various life experiences, becomes an invaluable asset when pursuing ambitious goals, especially later in life. It provides the fortitude to persevere through difficulties, to adapt to changing circumstances, and to maintain a positive outlook even when facing setbacks. This resilience acts as a buffer against discouragement and provides the mental toughness required to stay committed to a vision.

A lifetime of experiences provides a deep understanding of oneself—one's strengths, weaknesses, values, passions, and motivations. This self-knowledge is crucial for making informed decisions about one's future and for pursuing goals that are truly aligned with personal values and interests. It allows individuals to leverage their strengths effectively, to manage their weaknesses strategically, and to pursue paths that are genuinely fulfilling. This level of self-awareness is often a key differentiator in achieving meaningful and lasting success.

Crystallized Intelligence refers to the accumulation of knowledge, skills, and experience over time. Unlike fluid intelligence, which is associated with problem-solving and abstract reasoning, crystallized intelligence continues to grow throughout adulthood. This accumulated knowledge base provides a rich foundation for learning new things, making connections between seemingly disparate concepts, and applying past experiences to new situations. It's the wisdom that comes from years of learning and applying knowledge in real-world contexts.

These qualities, honed over a lifetime, offer several distinct advantages for those pursuing new endeavours later in life. The combination of accumulated wisdom and self-knowledge provides a unique perspective that can be invaluable in creative endeavours, problem-solving, and leadership roles. This perspective allows individuals to see things from a different angle, to identify opportunities that others might miss, and to approach challenges with greater insight and understanding.

Life experience provides a richer understanding of human nature, societal dynamics, and the complexities of the world. This deeper understanding allows individuals to navigate complex situations more effectively, to build stronger relationships, and to make more informed decisions.

The resilience developed through overcoming past challenges provides the emotional fortitude to persevere through difficulties and maintain a long-term vision. This emotional strength is crucial for navigating setbacks, managing stress, and staying committed to goals, even when faced with obstacles.

These combined advantages create a powerful foundation for late-life achievement. They demonstrate that the later stages of life are not a period of decline but rather a time of immense potential, fueled by the rich resources of experience. This accumulated wisdom, resilience, self-knowledge, and crystallized intelligence provide a unique and powerful advantage, allowing individuals to pursue their passions with greater clarity, purpose, and determination. They are not starting from scratch; they are building upon a lifetime of experiences, transforming the later years into a period of profound growth, fulfillment, and meaningful contribution.

The profiles we explored–Ray Kroc, Diana Nyad, Colonel Sanders, Grandma Moses, Stan Lee, Fauja Singh, Jessica Tandy, Henry Ford, and Betty White–each offered a unique perspective on the theme of late-life achievement. They demonstrated that success can manifest in countless forms, whether it's building a global business, conquering a physical challenge, creating art that resonates with millions, or simply finding new meaning and purpose in later years.

These individuals, while diverse in their pursuits, shared a common thread: an unwavering persistence, a strong sense of purpose, adaptability, self-belief, a commitment to learning and growth, strong support systems, and a genuine passion for their work. These qualities, as we explored in the previous chapter, are not exclusive to extraordinary individuals. They are qualities that we can all cultivate in our own lives.

This book does not shy away from the realities of aging. It doesn't attempt to paint an unrealistic picture where the natural processes of physical and cognitive change simply cease to exist. To do so would be disingenuous and ultimately unhelpful. Instead, its core purpose is to offer a crucial reframing of our perspective on aging, shifting away from the dominant narrative of decline and decay toward a more nuanced and empowering understanding. This reframing centers on recognizing that aging is not merely a process of diminishing capacities but a profound period of transformation, a time ripe with new beginnings and renewed possibilities. It's about acknowledging that while some aspects of our physical or cognitive abilities may change over time, our potential as human beings does not diminish; it simply evolves, taking on new forms and expressing itself in different ways.

The conventional view of aging often focuses on loss: loss of physical strength, loss of memory, loss of independence, and loss of opportunities. This deficit-based model paints a bleak picture, suggesting that the later years of life are primarily characterized by decline and deterioration. This perspective can be deeply disempowering, leading to feelings of fear, anxiety, and a sense of resignation to a diminished future. However, this book challenges this limited view, offering a more holistic and empowering perspective.

The reframing proposed here emphasizes that aging is a process of continuous development, albeit one that involves changes in various domains. While some physical and cognitive functions may decline, other aspects of our being, such as wisdom, emotional intelligence, and self-knowledge, continue to grow and deepen. This transformation is not about replacing one set of abilities with another; it's about the evolution of our potential, the emergence of new strengths and capacities that are uniquely suited to this stage of life.

As we age, our priorities often shift. We may move away from the pursuit of external markers of success, such as career advancement or material wealth, and toward more intrinsic values, such as meaningful relationships, personal growth, and contributing to something larger than ourselves. This shift in priorities can open up new avenues for fulfillment and purpose.

Life experience cultivates a deeper understanding of oneself–one's values, passions, strengths, and weaknesses. This self-awareness allows for more intentional choices and a greater focus on activities that are truly aligned with personal values. Aging provides the opportunity to explore new interests, develop new skills, and pursue passions that may have been neglected in earlier years. This can lead to unexpected discoveries, new sources of joy, and a renewed sense of purpose.

The later years of life can be a time of significant contribution to society. With accumulated wisdom and experience, older adults can mentor younger generations, engage in community service, and advocate for important causes. This contributes not only to the well-being of society but also to a sense of purpose and fulfillment for the individual.

For many, later life provides the time and space to explore creative pursuits that may have been put on hold earlier in life. This can lead to the discovery of hidden talents, new forms of self-expression, and a greater sense of personal fulfillment.

This book celebrates this transformative aspect of aging. It's about recognizing that while some things may change, our capacity for growth, learning, and contribution remains vibrant. It's about understanding that our potential doesn't simply disappear; it transforms, evolving into new forms of expression and offering new opportunities for meaning and purpose. It's about embracing the later years of life not as a period of decline but as a time of profound transformation, a time for new beginnings, renewed possibilities, and the continued unfolding of our unique human potential. It emphasizes that this stage of life is not a closing chapter, but rather a new volume waiting to be written, filled with unique stories, experiences, and contributions.

The concept of the "Unexpected Bloom," the emergence of talent, passion, or purpose later in life, is a central theme of this book. It challenges us to look beyond conventional timelines and embrace the possibility of discovering new passions and achieving great things at any stage of life. It reminds us that the human spirit is capable of remarkable resilience and that creativity can flourish at any age.

So, how can you apply the lessons learned from these extraordinary lives to your own journey? How can you find your own "Unexpected Bloom"?

First, reject the Time Trap. Let go of the self-imposed deadlines and societal pressures that tell you there's a "right" time for everything. Embrace the idea that your journey is unique and that your potential is not limited by your age.

Second, embrace the advantages of experience. Recognize the value of your accumulated wisdom, resilience, and self-knowledge. These qualities are powerful assets in pursuing your goals.

Third, find your fire. Take the time to explore your interests, identify your passions, and reconnect with your inner voice. Ask yourself the fundamental questions: What did I love doing as a child? What am I naturally good at? What problems do I care about solving? What activities make me feel energized and alive?

Fourth, build your bridge. Develop strategies for overcoming the obstacles that may stand in your way. Manage your fears, challenge your self-doubt, prioritize your time, and build a strong support system.

Fifth, take the leap. Translate your passions and plans into action. Start small, create a routine, track your progress, and embrace a growth mindset. Remember that setbacks are inevitable, but they are also opportunities for learning and growth.

Finally, cultivate the qualities of extraordinary individuals. Embrace persistence, find your purpose, adapt to change, believe in yourself, commit to lifelong learning, build strong relationships, and pursue your passions with genuine enthusiasm.

The overarching message woven throughout these pages culminates in a powerful and liberating truth: life is not a race to a predetermined finish line; it is a journey of continuous growth, ongoing discovery, and ever-present possibility. This fundamental shift in perspective frees us from the constraints of artificial timelines and societal expectations, allowing us to embrace the full spectrum of life's potential at every stage. It rejects the notion of a singular peak or a limited window of opportunity, instead emphasizing the ongoing capacity for development, reinvention, and meaningful contribution.

This perspective challenges the common misconception that life is a linear progression with a defined endpoint, a race against time where the goal is to achieve everything by a certain age. This "race" mentality fosters anxiety, comparison, and a sense of inadequacy when individuals feel they are "falling behind" or not meeting external benchmarks. However, by understanding life as a continuous journey, we liberate ourselves from this pressure and embrace the unfolding narrative of our own unique experiences.

The individuals profiled in this book serve as compelling examples of this principle. Their stories are not tales of early bloomers reaching their peak and then fading away; they are narratives of individuals who found new purpose, ignited long-dormant passions, and achieved remarkable feats at various stages of life, often well beyond what society deems the "prime" years. They have shown us, through their lived experiences, that it's never too late to begin a new chapter, to pursue a long-held dream, or to make a significant difference in the world. Whether it's starting a business in one's 50s, embarking on a challenging physical endeavour in one's 60s, or discovering a creative talent in one's 70s, these stories demonstrate that the potential for growth and achievement is not bound by age.

Their journeys are testaments to the enduring power of the human spirit–the innate capacity for resilience, adaptation, and the unwavering pursuit of meaning and purpose. They embody the idea that the human spirit is not a static entity but a dynamic force capable of constant renewal and transformation. They remind us that even after facing setbacks, disappointments, or periods of stagnation, we retain the capacity to reinvent ourselves, to discover new passions, and to contribute to the world in meaningful ways.

These narratives offer a powerful reminder that one life, lived with purpose and passion, is indeed never too late. This emphasis on purpose and passion is crucial. It's not simply about filling the later years with activities; it's about finding activities that resonate deeply with our values, ignite our inner fire, and provide a sense of meaning and fulfillment. When we align our actions with our passions, we tap into a powerful source of motivation that sustains us through challenges and propels us toward our goals.

The metaphor of the unfolding canvas encapsulates this idea perfectly. Life is not a pre-painted picture with a fixed image; it is an ever-evolving canvas, constantly presenting new opportunities for creation, exploration, and self-expression. The colours we choose, the brushstrokes we make, and the images we create are not dictated by a predetermined pattern; they are shaped by our experiences, our choices, and our evolving understanding of ourselves and the world. The canvas of your life is still unfolding, offering infinite possibilities for growth, discovery, and creation. Embrace these possibilities with open arms, ignite your inner fire with passion and purpose, and create your own unique masterpiece. The journey is not about reaching a specific destination; it's about the continuous act of creating, learning, and becoming, a process that continues throughout the entire lifespan.

Acknowledgements

This book wouldn't exist without the support and encouragement of many incredible individuals. First and foremost, I want to express my deepest gratitude to my family, whose unwavering love and support have been my constant source of strength throughout this journey.

To my parents, thank you for nurturing my curiosity, fostering my love of learning, and always encouraging me to pursue my passions. Your unwavering belief in me, even when I doubted myself, has been a constant source of inspiration. I am forever grateful for the values you instilled in me: the importance of hard work, the value of kindness, and the courage to embrace new challenges.

To my brother Praveen Gaurav, thank you for your constant companionship, your playful banter, and your unwavering support. You have been my closest confidante, my sounding board, and my greatest cheerleader. I cherish the memories we've shared, the laughter we've enjoyed, and the unwavering bond we share.

A special thanks to my partner, who likes to call herself Rajmata, for her unwavering love, support, and belief in me. Your patience, encouragement, and constant support have been my anchor during the challenging times and my greatest source of joy during the triumphs. Thank you for always believing in me, even when I doubted myself. Your love has been my greatest source of strength and inspiration throughout this journey.

To my friends, thank you for your insightful feedback, your honest critiques, and your unwavering belief in me. Your laughter, your encouragement, and your unwavering support have been a constant source of strength and inspiration throughout this process. I cherish the memories we've shared, the deep conversations we've had, and the unwavering support you've offered during both the highs and lows of this journey. I am truly blessed to have such wonderful friends in my life.

I am deeply indebted to my superiors whose wisdom and guidance have shaped my thinking and inspired my writing. Your insightful feedback, challenging questions, and unwavering support have been instrumental in my growth as a writer. I am forever grateful for your belief in my potential and for the profound impact you have had on my journey.

I would also like to express my sincere gratitude to my publisher, Astitva Prakashan for their invaluable contributions to this book. Your expertise and dedication have been instrumental in bringing this book to life, and I am incredibly grateful for your partnership.

To the countless individuals who have shared their stories of personal growth and rediscovery with me, thank you for your openness, honesty, and willingness to share your experiences. Your stories have deeply moved and inspired me, and they have enriched this book in countless ways. Your vulnerability, your courage, and your unwavering spirit have been a constant source of inspiration throughout my writing process.

I would also like to acknowledge the countless hours of research, reading, and reflection that have gone into the creation of this book. I am grateful for the opportunity to delve deep into the world of human potential and to explore the profound impact of pursuing one's passions and embracing new experiences throughout the lifespan.

Finally, I want to express my gratitude to myself for believing in this project, for persevering through the challenges, and for never giving up on my dream of sharing this message with the world. This book is a testament to the power of perseverance, the importance of embracing change, and the endless possibilities that exist at every stage of life. It is a reminder that it is never too late to pursue our dreams, to rediscover our passions, and to live a life of purpose and fulfillment.

This book is dedicated to all those who believe that it is never too late to embrace new beginnings, to challenge societal expectations, and to live a life of purpose and fulfillment. To those who dare to dream big, to those who embrace the journey of self-discovery, and to those who continue to learn and grow throughout their lives.

Thank you all.